P9-CKT-335

HAYS, H. R., ed.   12 Spanish American poets; an anthology, tr., notes, and intro. by the editor.   Beacon, 1972 (orig. pub. by Yale, 1943). 336p bibl 72-75538. 12.50, 3.95 pa.   ISBN 0-8070-6396-7
This reissue will be most useful to the student of Spanish American poetry who has only average knowledge of the language. Some of the most important representatives of a literary genre in which so many artists of the various countries excel were chosen for this anthology. The translator does more than simply translate — he catches the mood and tone of each one of the 12 poets, giving a truly poetic English version of a wide variety of poems. Hays is well aware of the musical quality of many of the poems, likewise of the great number of verse patterns, and he succeeds in his English version to recreate each author's special qualities. The translation does justice to poetic prose, to popular verse, and to surrealism. An introduction and notes on each individual poet make this book attractive and informative.

PUBLISHED ON THE
FOUNDATION ESTABLISHED IN MEMORY OF
OLIVER BATY CUNNINGHAM
OF THE CLASS OF 1917
YALE COLLEGE

12
SPANISH AMERICAN POETS

AN ANTHOLOGY

EDITED BY H. R. HAYS

ENGLISH TRANSLATIONS, NOTES, AND
INTRODUCTION BY THE EDITOR

LIBRARY

UNIVERSITY OF

NEW HAVEN
YALE UNIVERSITY PRESS
LONDON · HUMPHREY MILFORD · OXFORD UNIVERSITY PRESS
1943

Copyright, 1943, by Yale University Press

Printed in the United States of America

First published, September, 1943
Second printing, November, 1943

All rights reserved. This book may not be
reproduced, in whole or in part, in any form
(except by reviewers for the public press),
without written permission from the publishers.

LIBRARY
APR 28 1972
UNIVERSITY OF THE PACIFIC

247706

The Oliver Baty Cunningham

Memorial Publication

Fund

The present volume is the nineteenth work published by the
Yale University Press on the Oliver Baty Cunningham Me-
morial Publication Fund. This Foundation was established
May 8, 1920, by a gift from Frank S. Cunningham, Esq., of
Chicago, to Yale University, in memory of his son, Captain
Oliver Baty Cunningham, 15th United States Field Artillery,
who was born in Chicago, September 17, 1894, and was
graduated from Yale College in the Class of 1917. As an
undergraduate he was distinguished alike for high scholar-
ship and for proved capacity in leadership among his fel-
lows, as evidenced by his selection as Gordon Brown Prize
Man from his class. He received his commission as Second
Lieutenant, United States Field Artillery, at the First Offi-
cers' Training Camp at Fort Sheridan, and in December,
1917, was detailed abroad for service, receiving subse-
quently the Distinguished Service Medal. He was killed
while on active duty near Thiaucourt, France, on Sep-
tember 17, 1918, the twenty-fourth anniversary of his birth.

ACKNOWLEDGMENT

THE editor wishes to express his thanks to Jorge Carrera Andrade, consul general for Ecuador in San Francisco, to Manuel Moreno Jimeno of Lima, to Andrés Iduarte and Eugenio Florit of Columbia University, to Miss Angélica Mendoza of Sarah Lawrence College for their advice and assistance in preparing this anthology. To José Juan Arrom of Yale University, who gave generously of his time in consultation and advice, he is particularly indebted.

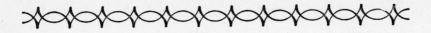

CONTENTS

CONTENTS

CONTENTS

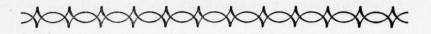

1.

POETRY AND
LATIN AMERICAN CULTURE

IN order to understand the poetry of the Spanish American peoples of that huge area embracing Mexico, Central and South America, and the Caribbean islands, one must realize what fundamental differences separate this culture from that of the United States. Although Latin America had universities and the beginning of a literature almost a hundred years before North America had them, its economic and social development, as a result of geographical and political obstacles, has been retarded and today the industrial revolution is still going on. As a result, the population is clustered here and there in a few urban centers while vast areas are hardly settled at all, and between these population centers there is often very limited communication. On the other hand national boundaries are sometimes artificial, and whole sections which are divided into separate nations are racially, economically, and culturally similar.

All this makes for a contradictory situation. While on the one hand regionalism flourishes and national pride seeks for indigenous artistic expression, on the other we find movements and trends which produce almost the same literary phenomena in various parts of the southern continent. Peru, Ecuador, and Bolivia, for instance, have a common heritage of ancient Andean culture. Uruguay and Argentina have a predominantly European population and they have had closer economic connections with the European continent than with other portions of Latin America.

Likewise, in respect to poetry, we find both individual national schools and, at the same time, a good deal of cultural interchange. And since Spanish is the language which unites the majority of the republics, there is really one poetic literature to which first one country, then another, makes a contribution which affects the course of the movement.

Within the countries themselves there are highly diverse elements which have prevented political stability and the formation of a homogeneous national outlook. The impact of individualistic Spaniards upon the communally organized Indians in some countries, of Christianity upon paganism, a feudalism in which Spanish landowners exploited laborers of another race, all these sources of antagonism have hindered the development of a unified civilization such as our industrial economy has brought about in the United States. In consequence, Latin American intellectuals have felt themselves isolated. Their literate public was very small, their artistic milieu limited and provincial. They continued to look to European cultural centers for stimulus and inspiration. The small well-to-do bourgeoisie which produced some of the poets sent its children to Europe to complete their education. And the list of Spanish American expatriates is a long one—expatriates for both political and artistic reasons.

There has, of course, been a similar situation in the United States. We, too, have inherited certain attitudes as a result of the colonial relationship. We have alternately imitated European models and then repudiated them. But, during the nineteenth century, there were periods in our poetry when it was somewhat apart from the main stream of European writing and our twentieth-century renaissance involved a rediscovery of continental values.

Latin America, however, has kept a closer contact with European movements. Its poetry has inherited a more profound feeling of literary tradition, a greater sensitivity to world literature, and it has maintained a more sophisticated artistic attitude.

In world literature the full development of the novel seems to coincide with a complexly integrated industrial society. Such a society provides a firm texture of relationships and social forms which are good material for extended prose narrative and it also provides a large literate audience for the drama. Spanish America is relatively weak in dramatic literature. While it has produced distinguished novels, the best of them are soil novels—stories of the countryside, the ranches, and the plantations. And even in these novels it is remarkable how much lyricism is embedded in their structure. In many cases, too, the novelist is also a poet or has written poetry before turning to fiction. It is perhaps not too much to say that, measured by international standards, Spanish American literary achievement is greatest in the field of poetry.

It would seem that the feudal mixture of primitive masses leavened by a small intellectual class helps to account for this fact. The character of the settlements in South America, too—scanty population groups surrounded by great mountains and forests—would tend to make the writer aware of nature and himself. Since economic development has been retarded, men's minds have not been occupied with exploiting the resources of the continent. Instead, a vast and primitive new world has continued to dwarf the handful of Europeans who conquered it. The pampas, the cordilleras, and the jungles of the Amazon embrace the very suburbs of the cities. In such an atmosphere loneliness and introspection are a frequent literary mood and poetry seems to be the natural form of expression.

In actual style this body of poetry is conditioned by the world movements which have influenced it, but roughly three general attitudes have been evident in recent decades. There is, first, the complete withdrawal from anything local, poetry which is really a part of European literature. Then there is poetry concerned with provincial life in which the writer generally expresses his dissatisfaction with the sterility and poverty of his environment. Finally, there is the attempt to make use of national characteristics, which involves the use of local color and folklore.

The position of poets in Latin America is likewise different from that of their fellow writers in the United States. While it would be difficult to prove that poetry is more widely read, a greater percentage of educated people have tried their hand at writing it. The scores of anthologies packed with names are proof of a great amount of poetic activity. The large number of important poets who hold government positions or who function in the diplomatic and consular services of Latin America is undeniable evidence of the respect in which poets are held. Latin American governments—even some of the most reactionary dictatorships—have felt a responsibility toward their literary men and have made a practice of providing them with such positions. Since the duties are seldom onerous, this amounts to a kind of subsidizing of literary production. The writers who hold such posts travel in foreign countries and come in contact with new ideas. This fact also helps to account for the cosmopolitan character of contemporary Spanish American poetry.

Certainly what might be termed the "frontier attitude" toward poetry is entirely lacking—that attitude engendered by the rapidly expanding commercialism and industrial exploitation of North America, now somewhat modified, that the arts are an effete and useless activity chiefly suitable to amuse women. The slower tempo of living in the southern hemisphere, a civilization, in short, still more closely attuned to an agricultural rhythm than to that of the machine, is more sympathetic to an art which requires leisure and contemplation.

Poetry in Latin America is therefore a more significant cultural expression than it is in the United States. From it we may become familiar with the character of the people, their particular kinds of sensitivity, their ways of thinking and feeling.

2.

THE SYMBOLIST HERITAGE

ODERN Spanish American poetry is generally considered to begin with Rubén Darío. And significantly enough, the work of this Nicaraguan also marks a turning point in Spanish letters. From his time on, Spanish America challenges Spain for leadership in poetry.

Darío brought symbolism into Spanish poetry. The romantic movement had not reached a high point of development in the new world, it was time for it to give way to a new poetic impulse. With the publication of *Azure* in 1888, the new poetic trend found expression in the verse and prose of Darío.

From the vantage point of the present it is possible to see that symbolism, originating in France toward the end of the nineteenth century, was the next world wide movement of poetic renewal after English romanticism. It came to full flower in Spain and Latin America later than in France. In the 'eighties Darío's work was more parnassian than symbolist and it was not until the end of the century that he wrote truly symbolist verses. The generation of poets who sprang up under his influence and developed what was called the "modernist" movement in Spanish America were doing their best work in the 'nineties and the early decades of the twentieth century.

The modernist movement proper (according to Federico de Onís) extended from 1896 to 1905. The importance of modernism in Spanish literature cannot be underestimated. It was the first revolutionary literary movement in the southern republics and also one of the first symptoms of the awakening of a new culture. Certain parnassian and romantic elements still persisted in the modernist style; there were excursions into gothicism, popular ballads and the Spanish Golden

Age, but as a whole the movement had a symbolist tone and
can be considered the Spanish branch of the symbolist move-
ment.

The same social impulse is discernible in both the roman-
tic and symbolist movements—a feeling of dissatisfaction
and rebellion against the existing order. The romantic revolt,
however, is a moral revolution; it tends to be dramatic, the
individual is still in contact with society deliberately flouting
its laws. The parnassian emphasis on form and plasticity al-
ready indicates a shift from moral indignation to aristocratic
aloofness. Finally the symbolist reaction against society dei-
fies the artist. The individual now exists for himself alone; he
has broken his connection with the existing order to live in
his own world of sensation and his own consciousness is
what interests him most.

As has been earlier pointed out, the social situation in
Spanish America was especially likely to create the isolated
individualist. There had already been precursors of the sym-
bolist mood such as José Asunción Silva of Colombia and
Manuel Gutiérrez Nájera of Mexico, but it was Darío who
crystalized the modernist style. He imported French literary
symbols, widened Spanish poetic diction, modified tradi-
tional metrics, revived old verse forms and brought musical-
ity to the point where it overshadowed content. He also pop-
ularized the cult of beauty as an end in itself. Since he was
highly gifted and traveled widely and wrote prolifically, his
influence spread all over Spanish America and caused a ren-
aissance in Spanish poetry as well.

The early phase of the modernist movement was therefore
exotic and precious. It was followed by a reaction which has
been called postmodernism or *mundonovismo,* new world-
ism. New worldism was the Spanish American expression of
a tendency which is inherent in the whole symbolist move-
ment, a tendency which runs through the whole modern pe-
riod of artistic disorientation. The reaction to the modernist
movement revealed a dualism in the realm of the spirit, a
split in the nature of the modern artist which cannot be

healed until conditions are such that he once more becomes an integral part of society.

It is possible to express dissatisfaction with one's environment either by withdrawing into fantasy and creating something better or by rendering the environment faithfully and holding it up to scorn. Symbolism and naturalism have run a parallel course, often becoming inextricably blended. The symbolist poet in his preoccupation with the most precise rendering of sense impressions sometimes brought the traditionally unpoetic into poetry. This tendency furnished a basis for the reaction to the early modernist movement. The new worldists rebelled against the French style, the cult of beauty, and the preciosity of their predecessors. They wished to write truly American poetry and therefore began to employ material from their daily experience. They drew on local color and frankly prosaic detail.

In attempting to create a new-world poetry some writers also turned to Spanish American history and local tradition. Most conspicuous of these was the Peruvian, Santos Chocano, who wrote of the conquistadors and Incas in a would-be epic style. This, however, was not entirely new. The romantics had already exploited the picturesque side of history and, since the impulse to use local incident and tradition accompanies each upsurge of nationalism, it is a familiar characteristic of Spanish American literature rather than the product of a particular school. On the whole, it was the realistic element which differentiated the postmodernists from the founders of the movement.

New worldism did not entirely drive out modernism. The two trends existed side by side and continued to develop, the former moving in the direction of naturalism and social criticism, the latter toward even more personal forms of expression; and when both appear in the work of the same writer, they can be seen most clearly as two facets of the same general trend. For example, the Uruguayan, Herrera y Reissig, who is generally considered a postmodernist, published the following stanzas in 1906.

La druídica pompa de las selvas se cubre
De una gótica herrumbre de silencio y estragos;
Y Cibeles esquiva su balsámica ubre,
Con un hilo de lágrimas en los párpados vagos. . .

Sus cabellos de místico azafrán llora Octubre
En los lívidos ojos de muaré de los lagos.
Las cigüeñas exodan. Y los buhos aciagos
Ululúan la mofa de un presagio insalubre. . .

.   .   .   .   .

The druid pomp of the woods is covered over
With a gothic rust of silence and of ruin;
And Cybele withdraws her udder of balsam
With a thread of tears in her misty eyes. . .

October weeps her hair of mystical saffron
Into the lakes' livid eyes of rippled silk.
The storks depart. And the mournful owls
Moan a mockery of an omen of sickness. . .

This is typical of the modernist or symbolist mood. Although the poet deals with an actual landscape, the treatment is so subjective that it becomes a land of unreality, bathed in strange colors. The feeling of melancholy is enhanced by such elements as owls, weeping, and gothic rust. There is also something decadent in the suggestion of sickness and ruin. Finally such images as "udder of balsam," "saffron hair," "rust of silence," and "eyes of rippled silk" illustrate the striving for originality and freshness of diction characteristic of the modernists. This kind of writing stems from the modernist movement proper, but in the same collection Herrera was already publishing realistic verses representative of the postmodernist reaction.

LA SIESTA

No late más que un único reloj: el campanario,
Que cuenta los dichosos hastíos de la aldea,
El cual, al sol de enero, agriamente chispea,
Con su aspecto remoto de viejo refractario. . .

A la puerta, sentado se duerme el boticario. . .
En la plaza yacente la gallina cloquea
Y un tronco de ojaranzo arde en la chimenea,
Junto a la cual el cura medita su breviario.

Todo es paz en la casa. Un cielo sin rigores,
Bendice la faena, reparte los sudores. . .
Madres, hermanas, tías, cantan lavando en rueda

Las ropas que el domingo sufren los campesinos. . .
Y el asno vagabundo que ha entrado en la vereda
Huye, soltando coces, de los perros vecinos.

THE SIESTA

Only a single clock strikes: the one in the belltower,
Relating the village's happy boredoms,
The clock that sparkles sourly in January sunlight
With its distant look of an obstinate old man. . .

The apothecary sleeps, sitting in the doorway. . .
A hen is clucking in the vacant square
And a hornbeam log burns in the fireplace,
Beside it the priest ponders over his breviary.

All is peace in the house. A balmy sky
Blesses the work, distributes perspiration. . .
Mothers, daughters, aunts sing as, in a circle,

They wash the clothes that farmers endure on Sunday. . .
And the wandering donkey that has entered the path
Flies bucking and kicking from the dogs of the neighbors.

This sonnet is the antithesis of the lines quoted above.
Instead of bathing his landscape with mystical saffron, the
poet ironically notes down the dogs chasing a stray donkey
and the perspiring laundresses. All of the detail is precise.
The contrasting emotional tone is also significant. Here the
mood is somewhat mixed, verging on the sentimental but
with an ironic touch or two that indicates a critical attitude.
The criticism is also tinged with humor.

The two trends which have just been illustrated constitute the background of contemporary Spanish American poetry. Descriptive verse like the sonnet just quoted, initiated by the postmodernists, leads directly to the bitter satire of L. C. López of Colombia or to the nostalgic genre painting of the Mexican, López Velarde (poets with whose work this anthology begins). The modernist style proper also persists, mainly in countries which have not reacted to subsequent trends. But sybolism or moderism has never been completely ousted from Spanish American poetry. Its mood of delicate melancholy creeps back in new forms and in new disguises.

The lingering influence of modernism constitutes the most striking difference between North American and Spanish American poetry today. Since French symbolism affected the United States seriously only after 1910 and even then in highly modified form through such poets as Wallace Stevens, T. S. Eliot, and Marianne Moore, it has never become our academic style. Our more conventional poets tend to cling to the Victorian or Georgian style. In the background of our poetry there are still vestiges of naïve optimism, of homespun moralizing, of the Whitmanic disregard for artistic discipline. In contrast, even the most minor Spanish American versifier echoes a sophisticated artistic style and instinctively employs the symbols of European literary tradition.

3.

THE DECADES OF EXPERIMENT

THE first World War undoubtedly served as midwife to the literary revolution that followed symbolism. The attitude of delicate melancholy had hardened into a pose. Though capable of further refinement by such poets as Valéry, it had to give way before new intellectual and emotional points of view. Paris remained the center of cultural ferment and, even before the war was over, certain precursors were experimenting with new kinds of fantasy. Apollinaire's *Calligrammes* was written between 1913 and 1916. In this book we find typographical novelties and unusual imagery. Cocteau's *Le Potomak*, written during 1913 and 1914, already introduced the dream world he has been inhabiting ever since. This early experimental movement crystallized around the publication *Nord Sud* in 1917 and, led by Apollinaire, the poets allied themselves with the artists of the period and called themselves cubists. The most noteworthy break which the new poetry made with the past was the abandonment of the anecdote. The latter had already become tenuous and almost invisible in such symbolist poetry as that of Mallarmé but the cubist poem was a succession of superimposed annotations and reflections without causal connection. There was a conscious rejection of intellectual elements, a desire to achieve "pure lyricism." This paralleled the retreat of painting from representation; it was an attempt to do away with the accepted notion of reality and to discover, intuitively, a new kind of reality. This rejection of the anecdote as the basis of organization of the poem is a historic literary event. Practically all poetry written since has been affected by it.

Finally, in 1918, the publication *Dada* was founded, the same year that Jacque Vaché committed suicide, thus becoming a concrete symbol of this movement. Dada, though short-lived (it did not last more than three or four years), was literary rebellion pushed to the point of nihilism. The war had intensified the feeling that all must be changed, that everything existing must be swept away in favor of a spiritual and social renaissance. Since symbolism rejected all but the artist, dada did away with him. The simon-pure dadaist did not write at all and Vaché went as far as self-annihilation. To quote Emile Bouvier, "Dada became a warlike weapon the point of which was humor or, if you like, a warlike weapon for the demolition of the Old World by means of dynamite disguised as a simpleton's jest." The dadaist consciously wrote nonsense and organized meetings and lectures at which the public was ridiculed and insulted.

But writers cannot long cease to write. The originators of the movement (many of the same names crop up in cubism, dada, and the movements which follow) sought new directions, and in the decade which followed an orgy of experiment reigned. This experimental trend which affected both poetry and prose had its repercussions all over the world. In Spain it was called ultraism, in Chile creationism, in Germany expressionism, in Mexico stridentism, and in France, which continued to be in the vanguard, it simmered down to surrealism which has persisted up to the present.

Two characteristics continued to underlie this writing during the 'twenties, the abandonment of logical construction for the free association of ideas and images, and the rejection of traditional literary forms. Much of the verse written around 1918 glorifies the machine, the new age of science, sport, jazz, primitivism, hyperbolic new horizons. Apollinaire, the cubist, Guillermo de Torre, the Spanish ultraist, Huidobro, the creationist, Cendrars, the French vanguardist, all wrote poems to the Eiffel Tower, using it as a symbol of modernity. Curiously enough, this era of enthusiasm took something from Walt Whitman. "Give me your hand, Whitman," says Guillermo de Torre. What the vanguardists borrowed from the American poet was mainly an undisciplined excitement, the high pressure outburst, the loose ecstatic line, and they grafted to this their own violent imagery and sprinkled the result over the page in various type faces. These typographical tricks were not entirely silly. Nowadays poetry is more often read than recited aloud. In consequence line arrangement can create certain visual rhythms. The moment a poem is divided into stanzas the writer has begun to exploit visual arrangement. The vanguardists developed the principle and tossed words and phrases about to create an effect of excitement or in an attempt to achieve "simultaneity." The Argentinian, Borges, writes that Spanish ultraism is "reduction of the lyric to its primordial element, the metaphor. Cutting out inter-

mediate phrases, connective and useless adjectives. . . . .
Ultraist poems consist, then, of a series of metaphors, each
one of which contains its own suggestive quality and sum-
marizes an unedited vision of some fragment of life."

This first period of experimentalism ran its course rapidly.
The world had not changed as much as the younger literary
generation hoped it would. Their hysterical optimism evapo-
rated and they soon found themselves in the same situation
as their symbolist ancestors. They were faced with the
same dilemma that plagued the nineteenth century; they
either had to change the world or create new worlds of
their own. Left over from dada and all the other isms was
free association and a new extension of the use of the
image. André Breton and Louis Aragon, using the work of
Freud as a philosophic justification, launched the first
surrealist manifesto in 1924.

Surrealism posited the new reality and the new world
order in the subconscious of the artist. The surrealists car-
ried free association still further and aimed at the instinc-
tive organization of the dream. Their ultimate ideal was
automatic writing. In essence this was not so far from the
symbolists and in fact the new movement hailed Rimbaud,
particularly Rimbaud of the hallucinated "Bateau ivre," as
their literary ancestor. That they also resurrected the
French romantics, Lautréamont and Baudelaire, shows how
the tradition of romantic revolt has continued unbroken
from the nineteenth century to the present day.

Finally the movement publicly acknowledged its social
implications in 1930 when the second manifesto announced
the acceptance of Marxian dialectics.

Actually there has always been an element of subconscious
association in poetry. The imagination brings together two
hitherto unrelated concepts and creates a metaphor. The
emotional effect of poetic imagery can never be entirely ana-
lyzed by the intellect—in short, there is always something
mystical in the poetic process. The surrealists, however, re-
jected the literary patterns and the intellectual structure

which have traditionally molded the imaginative material into artistic forms.

In one important point the surrealists differed from their symbolist predecessors. They repeatedly announced the need for new myths, for new imaginative concepts around which to organize man's spiritual life. In fact they hoped to find them in their dreams. Probably this groping for new myths is the most valuable contribution that surrealism has made.

The emotional tone of true surrealist poetry also differs from that of symbolism. While the latter was steeped in melancholy, the sad loneliness of rejection, surrealism is full of grotesque humor, surprise, and sadistic violence.

In Latin America the different phases of the experimental movement did not follow each other in orderly sequence. There was no real dada poetry. Ultraist and surrealist tendencies occur side by side. The new ferment affected some countries much later than others and in a few cases there has been no violent break with modernism at all. In most cases, however, after the first World War, Spanish American intellectuals had begun to feel that modernism and postmodernism had lost their vitality. The subsequent poetic revolutions never assumed the unified character of modernism, perhaps because no new Darío arose to give ideological leadership to the new poetry. Actually, the experimental trend has been modified by various local forces; the cult of the Indian native, social protest, or new forms of nationalism. Because, no doubt, of its continuing importance in painting and Breton's activity as a theorist—launching manifestoes and reviews—surrealism has shown the most vitality. In Mexico the *Ulises* group practiced surrealism in the early 'twenties; the group associated with the publication *Amauta* in Peru was influenced by it in the early 'thirties and many of the younger Peruvians are definitely surrealists. The *Viernes* group of Venezuela, founded in 1936, also uses surrealist devices. In Uruguay Roberto Ibáñez, the leader of the movement called transcreationism, is also a semi-surrealist. In fact in nearly every Spanish American country which is active poetically there are at least individual poets whose work is somewhat affected by this school.

It is true that the most important Spanish American poets are not orthodox surrealists. Once again it is not possible to draw a hard-and-fast line between different trends. The contemporary poets of South America sometimes carry on the symbolist or modernist mood and blend it with associative technique. Or they at times use fairly realistic material and distort it until it assumes a dream quality. In any case surrealism in Latin America has never been regarded as crackpot nonsense. It has never been treated with suspicion as in Anglo-American literature. The major poets have not hesitated to borrow something from the movement. Its acceptance and continuing practice are one more proof of the more intimate connection between European literature and that of Spanish America.

4.

NEW TYPES OF OBJECTIVITY

ALONGSIDE the two general trends just sketched, there is discernible a new desire for affirmation in Spanish American poetry. This cannot be summed up in a single movement; it is less a literary style than an emotional reaction toward the contemporary world. Several widely differing causes contribute to it—intrinsically it reflects the deepening political crisis of the 'thirties. What might be called the new objectivity has its relation to the dual attitude which was already present in the nineteenth century. While surrealism represents the negative side of the rebellion, the newer objectivity represents the positive pole, the attempt to grapple with life and, if not actively to change it, at least to participate in the struggle, to deal with heroic events, and to glorify more directly social ideals. In some cases, though not always, the latter attitude is affected by marxism; in every case it is coupled with a sympathy for the masses of the people and a desire to express their aspirations.

It is significant that today the social forces which modify literary movements have finally become explicit. Many poets who write in the surrealist style are politically radical and the surrealist leaders defend their position with dialectical arguments. The split nature of the modern artist has finally become a matter for critical discussion.

The intellectuals of Spanish America were profoundly affected by the Spanish Civil War. The majority of the leading poets were intensely sympathetic to the Republican cause and sincerely anti-Fascist. The war became a symbol of the struggle for human progress. Not being directly active in the conflict, these poets were able to write of it with a certain objectivity though with great intensity. Some of them even went to Spain and tried to help in various civilian capacities while the war was going on. Even such vanguardists as Pablo Neruda were moved to glorify the people's army. In consequence the war poems are not exactly a movement but rather a symptom or a forerunner of a trend which is still taking shape.

A more permanent element affecting the poetic impulse under discussion is the racial variety in the Latin American republics. According to the estimate of Preston James, half the population of Ecuador is full-blooded Indian. Hubert Herring has it 10 per cent white, 90 per cent Indian and mestizo. Peru, according to James, is half Indian with another 33 per cent mestizo, while Herring makes it 90 per cent Indian and mestizo and 10 per cent white. Both agree in estimating Venezuela as about 70 per cent mestizo with another 8 per cent Negro. James considers Mexico 30 per cent pure Indian with another 60 per cent mestizo; Herring believes that about three fourths of the population is Indian or mestizo. James estimates that 65 to 75 per cent of Chile is mestizo with prevailingly white blood. Herring calls it a white man's country with some Indian blood in nearly all the inhabitants. Herring describes Bolivia as nine tenths Indian and mestizo. In spite of the roughness of such estimates, they do give a concrete idea of the large portion of Spanish America's population which is non-European.

Since these countries were conquered by Europeans and the Negroes were imported as slaves, it is always the working class which is pure Indian or Negro or mestizo or mulatto. In recent years intellectuals have ceased to regard these primitive races as picturesque, and movements for social reform or revolution have sprung up under both native and white leadership. Together with social reform comes a reassertion of the cultural heritage of the primitive race which, in turn, stimulates a literary movement. In Peru, Ecuador, and Bolivia it is called indigenism. A similar trend also exists in Mexico but it finds literary expression in the novel rather than in poetry. Indigenist poetry varies in style; Peralta of Peru, for instance, uses typically ultraist metaphors. It is therefore not possible to describe this movement in literary terms; what identifies it is subject matter. It may draw on local color and folklore but it is not concerned with the merely picturesque. Its basic inspiration is always social.

Exactly paralleling this movement in the Caribbean islands, with Cuba as a center, there has been a strong movement based on the folklore and the racial characteristics of the Negroes and mulattoes who make up a large percentage of the population, the original Indians having long since disappeared. This Afro-Cuban school depends for its inspiration upon the primitive dance forms, legends, and popular songs which are current among the Antilles.

While the Andean civilization left no written literature and the Indian folksong seems to have had little influence on indigenist poetry, the Afro-Cuban or Afro-Spanish school has succeeded in incorporating some Negro dance–lyric forms, such as the rumba and the *son,* into the new poetry. In most of these cases of native literary cults it is probable that the European interest in primitive art has helped to form them and the discovery of cultural values in primitive races is not so indigenous as their proponents sometimes imply. In proof of this it might be pointed out that several of the leading "negrists," Ballagas and Palés Matos, for example, have no Negro blood in their veins at all. What form the influence of the non-European races upon Spanish American culture is going to take in the future is yet to be determined. It is clear, however, that the blending of races is rapidly continuing, and many of the writers of the future will be of mixed stock as, indeed, many of them already are today. To quote Uriel García, "Indians and conquistadors who enter the new and transformed American panorama create a culture which they mutually modify." Critics have written of a specific Indian melancholy and mystical resignation. But melancholy is also a symbolist characteristic. Much has also been made of Negro sensuality but the white writers of Afro-Spanish poetry have outdone the Negroes in eroticism. As yet, indigenist poetry seems to be poetry written *about* Indians rather than to be a profound expression of a racial sensitivity. Perhaps more truly Indian qualities can be found in poets of mixed blood who do not profess to be indigenists at all. Afro-Spanish poetry comes nearer to creating a new genre. But already the school begins to decline and its leading poet, Guillén, is writing ballads which are close to the Spanish tradition.

In any case, these trends are an expression of Latin America's coming of age politically and socially and of a desire to vindicate the masses of the people as a creative force. They are also an attempt to decentralize poetry and to shake the monopoly of the large Europeanized centers.

There is still another way in which the contemporary impulse to connect poetry with a wider audience is apparent. It is manifest in the search for more popular poetic techniques. The Spanish poet, Juan Ramón Jiménez, traces two lines in Spanish literature. The one which he calls popular, collective, and impulsive, he associates with the *Poema del*

Cid, Lope de Vega, Cervantes, Unamuno, and García Lorca; the other, individualistic and ecstatic, he illustrates with Góngora, Quevedo, Calderón, and Rubén Darío. He feels that the finest Spanish poetry of the past has been the product of a union of these two trends. Whether this point of view is valid or not, it is certainly true that contemporary Spanish poetry has made efforts to move in the direction of the popular and the collective. Lorca, in particular, revived traditional folk-ballad forms and an attempt has been made to see him as a poet of the people. But Lorca's poetry is full of fantastic, even surrealist elements. At the most he was perhaps striving to achieve the union of the two poetic lines of which Jiménez speaks.

In Spanish America a similar trend toward popular forms exists. In some cases under the influence of García Lorca, in other cases independently, a great number of Spanish American poets have experimented with the old Spanish *romance* or with the *corrido,* the folk form current in Mexico and South America. Guillén of Cuba has not only worked in the Cuban popular song forms but recently has written ballads somewhat reminiscent of Lorca. Poetry of this kind is, of course, simple in phrasing and strictly traditional in rhyme and meter. It is a reaction against the associative, antitraditional movement and a reassertion of the primitive function of poetry as song.

The foregoing summary is necessarily incomplete. It is impossible to do justice to the multiplicity of poetic currents or to synthesize adequately the characteristics of the poetic literatures of so many countries in a few pages. Critical studies of recent Spanish American poetry are fragmentary and tentative and precise historical data are difficult to obtain. In any case, generalizations about contemporary writing are dangerous. It is better to let the poems speak for themselves. From the movements just sketched it can at least be seen that a wide variety of poetic writing is now going on in the southern hemisphere and that this poetry is intensely alert to all the contemporary intellectual and emotional trends. Its imaginative richness is indisputable. It is a poetry of abundant imagery, sacrificing formal discipline at times to robustness, perfection of finish to spontaneity. It has inherited elegance and charm from France and Spain; it draws color from local tradition and folklore and, above all, it exhibits a freshness and a creative intensity that are characteristic of a culture which has recently developed self-awareness.

Now that the literature of Europe has, through fire and sword, received a setback from which it will take years to recover, the creative energy of Spanish America has become doubly precious. The poetic virility which is evident in the southern republics augurs well for the future.

5.

PURPOSE AND SCOPE OF THE ANTHOLOGY

THE present anthology makes no pretension to comprehensiveness. No attempt has been made to represent all the Spanish American republics since political boundaries are of geographical but not poetic importance. A dozen leading poets have been selected in order to give the reader a bird's-eye view of contemporary Spanish American poetry. The number has been rigorously limited so as to make possible the inclusion of a fair sample of each poet's work. In each case poems have been chosen to give an idea of the writer's development. There are many other poets of equal or nearly equal stature. The twelve included have been picked, first, because of their intrinsic poetic interest and, secondly, in order to represent the most important contemporary trends. They are also, in most cases, poets whose influence has been strongly felt.

The Mexican, Ramón López Velarde, though not a contemporary in time, has qualities which relate him to the present. He also represents the postmodernist movement at its best.

Symbolist or modernist elements are also present in the work of José Gorostiza, Jorge Carrera Andrade, the early work of Neruda; in fact, as has been said, almost every writer included has served his apprenticeship in the symbolist style.

Vicente Huidobro is one of the earliest links with the European vanguardist movement. Vallejo is also related to it. Borges was actually associated with the Spanish ultraists. Surrealism appears as an influence on Neruda, Fombona Pachano, and Pablo de Rokha. Some of Carrera Andrade's poems are indigenist. Nicolás Guillén represents the Afro-Cuban school. Both he and Pablo de Rokha are influenced by marxism. Gorostiza and Eugenio Florit are in feeling close to contemporary Spanish poetry. L. C. López and Borges are both poets of local color.

The translator has not attempted to rhyme poems which rhyme in the Spanish or to reproduce the original meters syllable by syllable since this inevitably results in padding and distortion. He has, however, tried to render the images faithfully and to preserve in every case the character of the original meter and to add nothing of his own. Translating into "equivalent meters" is often no better than a paraphrase. Even though the octosyllabic line is not common in English, turning it into anything else changes the character of the poem. It is hoped that the English versions preserve the spirit of the originals.

If this book can provide a glimpse of the poetic riches in the Spanish literature of the southern hemisphere, if it can stimulate in some measure further exploration in this poetic literature and help to increase the interest of the North American public in the culture of Latin America, it will have achieved its purpose.

RAMON LOPEZ VELARDE

b. 1888, Jerez, Mexico, d. 1921

RAMON LOPEZ VELARDE

b. 1888, Jerez, Mexico, d. 1921

L OPEZ VELARDE'S early education prepared him for an ecclesiastical career. Later he studied law, became a journalist, and held a position in the Mexican government. His contact with the Church, however, left its imprint upon everything he wrote. The intimate knowledge of Catholic ritual in which he was steeped in his formative years provided him with a poetic symbolism, a special language expressing the conflict within him between paganism and Christianity. Chronologically a postmodernist, his poetry is closely related to French symbolism. There are elements in his work that suggest the tender eroticism of Verlaine or the obscurity of Mallarmé, but such influences are blended with specifically Mexican material into highly original and subtle imagery. In the larger sense, the mixture of pagan and Christian emotions symbolizes the mixture of the two races in Mexico—dramatized in the combination of pagan ceremony with Christian tradition which can still be observed in popular festivals. And in this lies López Velarde's importance—his work sums up a number of Spanish American qualities which are even more clearly evident today than they were in his lifetime. His interpretation of racial virtues makes him a precursor of indigenism; he is an ironical poet of provincial life, he crystallizes certain nationalistic tendencies and, above all, his poetry is full of a warm sensuality which is truly Latin American. In addition, he is a fine technician, a master of musical effects, neologisms, and verbal color. During his lifetime his work was little read but contemporary critical judgment ranks him as one of the greatest poets Mexico has yet produced.

The long poem, "Suave patria," here included, was written in 1921, shortly before the poet's death. It is a kind of impressionist mural, a synthesis of all the qualities for which he loved his native land. It is probably as near as a symbolist poet could come to writing a national epic. Mexicans feel that this poem is one of the finest interpretations of the spirit of their country that has ever been written.

La sangre devota. Mexico City, 1916.
Zozobra. Mexico City, 1919.
El són del corazón. Mexico City, 1932.
Poemas escogidos (ed. by Xavier Villaurrutia). Mexico City, 1935.

MI PRIMA AGUEDA

Mi madrina invitaba a mi prima Agueda
a que pasara el día con nosotros,
y mi prima llegaba
con un contradictorio
prestigio de almidón y de temible
luto ceremonioso.

Agueda aparecía, resonante
de almidón, y sus ojos
verdes y sus mejillas rubicundas
me protegían contra el pavoroso
luto . . .

Yo era rapaz
y conocía la o por lo redondo,
y Agueda que tejía
mansa y perseverante en el sonoro
corredor, me causaba
calosfríos ignotos . . .

(Creo que hasta la debo la costumbre
heroicamente insana de hablar solo.)

A la hora de comer, en la penumbra
quieta del refectorio,
me iba embelesando un quebradizo
sonar intermitente de vajilla
y el timbre caricioso
de la voz de mi prima.

Agueda era
(luto, pupilas verdes y mejillas
rubicundas) un cesto policromo
de manzanas y uvas
en el ébano de un armario añoso.

La sangre devota (1916)

MY COUSIN AGUEDA

My godmother used to invite my cousin Agueda
To spend the day with us,
And my cousin came
With a contradictory
Aura of starch and of dreadful
Ceremonial mourning.

Agueda appeared, crackling
With starch, and her green eyes
And her rubicund cheeks
Protected me against the fearful
Mourning . . .

        I was a boy
And scarcely dry behind the ears,
And Agueda who was weaving
Meekly and perseveringly in the echoing
Corridor caused me
unknown chills . . .

(I believe I owe to her the heroically
Insane custom of talking to myself.)

At the dinner hour, in the quiet
Penumbra of the dining room,
I was enraptured by a brittle
Intermittent sound of tableware
And the tender tones
Of the voice of my cousin.

           Agueda
(Mourning, green pupils and rubicund
Cheeks) was a polichrome basket
Of apples and grapes
In the ebony of an aged cabinet.

NUESTRAS VIDAS SON
PENDULOS

¿Dónde estará la niña
que en aquel lugarejo
una noche de baile
me habló de sus deseos
de viajar y me dijo
su tedio?

Gemía el vals por ella
y ella era un boceto
lánguido: unos pendientes
de ámbar y un jasmín
en el pelo.

Gemían los violines
en el torpe quinteto . . .
E ignoraba la niña
que al quejarse de tedio
conmigo, se quejaba
con un péndulo.

Niña que me dijiste
en aquel lugarejo
una noche de baile
confidencias de tedio:
dondequiera que exhales
tu suspiro discreto,
nuestras vidas son péndulos . . .

Dos péndulos distantes
que oscilan paralelos
en una misma bruma
de invierno.

La sangre devota

OUR LIVES ARE PENDULUMS

Where will the girl be
Who in that village
On the night of a dance
Spoke to me of her desire
To travel and told me
Of her boredom?

The waltz was moaning for her
And she was a languid illustration:
Some amber pendants and a jasmine
In her hair.

The violins were moaning
In the sluggish quintet . . .
And the girl did not know
That in lamenting her boredom with me
She was lamenting
With a pendulum.

Girl, who told me
In that village
On the night of a dance
Secrets of your boredom:
Wherever you exhale
Your prudent sigh,
Our lives are pendulums . . .

Two distant pendulums
That swing in parallel
In the same mist
Of winter.

HORMIGAS

A la cálida vida que transcurre canora
con garbo de mujer sin letras ni antifaces,
a la invicta belleza que salva y enamora,
responde, en la embriaguez de la encantada hora,
un encono de hormigas en mis venas voraces.

Fustigan el desmán del perenne hormigueo
el pozo del silencio y el enjambre del ruido,
la harina rebanada como doble trofeo
en los fértiles bustos, el Infierno en que creo,
el estertor final y el preludio del nido.

Mas luego mis hormigas me negarán su abrazo
y han de huir de mis pobres y trabajados dedos
cual se olvida en la arena un gélido bagazo;
y tu boca, que es cifra de eróticos denuedos,
tu boca, que es mi rúbrica, mi manjar y mi adorno,
tu boca, en que la lengua vibra asomada al mundo
como réproba llama saliéndose de un horno,
en una turbia fecha de cierzo gemebundo
en que ronde la luna porque robarte quiera,
ha de oler a sudario y a hierba machacada,
a droga y a responso, a pábilo y a cera.

Antes de que deserten mis hormigas, Amada,
déjalas caminar camino de tu boca
a que apuren los viáticos del sanguinario fruto
que desde sarracenos oasis me provoca.

Antes de que tus labios mueran, para mi luto,
dámelos en el crítico umbral del cementerio
como perfume y pan y tósigo y cauterio.

Zozobra (1919)

ANTS

To the warm life that musically passes
In the dress of a woman without veils or letters,
To the unconquered beauty that saves and enamors,
In the enchanted hour's intoxication,
In my ravenous veins a fester of ants replies.

In the well of silence and the multitude of noise,
The flour, sliced like a double trophy
In fertile bosoms; the Hell I believe in,
The last death rattle and the prelude of the nest
Lash the excess of the perpetual ant hill.

But then my ants deny me its embrace
And must fly from my poor and laboring fingers
Like a bit of cold refuse forgotten in the sand;
And your mouth which is emblem of erotic braveries,
Your mouth, my rubric, my food, my adornment
(Your mouth whose tongue quivers, thrust out at the world
Like a flame of perdition shooting out from an oven
In the murky time when the north wind is moaning,
When the moon skulks as it seeks to rob you),
Has to smell like shroud and crushed grasses,
Like drug and responsory, like wax and candlewick.

Before my ants desert me, Beloved,
Let them travel the way of your mouth
To drink the viaticums of the bloody fruit
Which provokes me from Saracenic oases.

Before your lips die, give them to me
For my mourning, in the critical arch of the cemetery,
As perfume and bread and poison and cautery.

EL SON DEL CORAZON

Una música íntima no cesa,
porque transida en un abrazo de oro
la Caridad con el Amor se besa.

¿Oyes el diapasón del corazón?
Oye en su nota múltiple el estrépito
de los que fueron y de los que son.

Mis hermanos de todas las centurias
reconocen en mí su pausa igual,
sus mismas quejas y sus propias furias.

Soy la fronda parlante en que se mece
el pecho germinal del bardo druida
con la selva por diosa y por querida.

Soy la alberca lumínica en que nada,
como perla debajo de una lente,
debajo de las linfas, Scherezada.

Y soy el suspirante cristianismo
al hojear las bienaventuranzas
de la virgen que fué mi catecismo.

Y la nueva delicia, que acomoda
sus hipnotismos de color de tango
al figurín y al precio de la moda.

La redondez de la Creación atrueno
cortejando a las hembras y a las cosas
con el clamor pagano y nazareno.

¡Oh Psiquis, oh mi alma: suena a són
moderno, a són de selva, a són de orgía
y a són mariano, el són del corazón!

El són del corazón (1932)

THE SOUND OF THE HEART

An intimate music never ceases,
Though fainting in a gold embrace
Charity and love complete their kiss.

Do you hear the heart's diapason?
Hear in its many-sounding note the din
Of those who were and those who are.

My brothers in all the centuries
Detect in me their own delays,
Their own complaints and their own furies.

I am the speaking foliage in which is rocked
The fruitful breast of druid bard
With the wood as goddess and as lover.

I am the luminous pool wherein,
Like a pearl beneath a lens,
Scheherazade swims beneath the waters.

I am sighing Christianity
Leafing the beatitudes
Of that virgin who was my catechism.

I am the new delight that matches
Its tango-colored hypnotism
To the dummy and the price of fashion.

I thunder the roundness of creation,
Wooing things and wooing woman
With a clamor Nazarene and pagan.

O Psyche, O my soul: ring with a modern sound,
A sound of forests, a sound of orgies
And a sound of Mary, a sound of the heart.

LA ASCENSION Y LA ASUNCION

Vive conmigo no sé qué mujer
invisible y perfecta, que me encumbra
en cada anochecer y amanecer.

Sobre caricaturas y parodias,
enlazado mi cuerpo con el suyo,
suben al cielo como dos custodias . . .

Dogma recíproco del corazón:
ser, por virtud ajena y virtud propia,
a un tiempo la Ascensión y la Asunción!

Su corazón de niebla y teología,
abrochado a mi rojo corazón,
translada, en una música estelar,
el Sacramento de la Eucaristía.

Vuela de incógnito el fantasma de yeso,
y cuando salimos del fin de la atmósfera,
me da medio perfil para su diálogo
y un cuarto de perfil para su beso . . .

Dios, que me ve que sin mujer no atino
en lo pequeño ni en lo grande, dióme
de ángel guardián un ángel femenino.

¡Gracias, Señor, por el inmenso don
que transfigura en vuelo la caída,
juntando, en la miseria de la vida,
a un tiempo la Ascensión y la Asunción!

El són del corazón

THE ASCENSION AND THE ASSUMPTION

There lives beside me here an unknown woman,
Invisible and perfect, who exalts me
With every sunset and with every dawn.

Above all caricatures and parodies,
My body with her own enlaced,
We rise to heaven like two hosts . . .

Reciprocal dogma of the heart:
Through its own virtue and through another's virtue
Ascension and Assumption both in one!

Her heart, theology and mist,
Buttoned to the redness of my heart,
Translates into starry music
The sacrament of the Eucharist.

The fantasm of plaster flies incognito,
And when we emerge from the atmosphere's end
She gives me half her profile with her dialogue,
A quarter with her kiss.

God, who sees that I, without a woman,
Accomplish nothing either great or small,
Gave me, as guardian angel, a feminine angel.

Lord, I am thankful for this mighty gift
By which the fall is turned into a flight,
A marriage in the midst of life's misfortunes,
Ascension and Assumption both in one!

SUAVE PATRIA

PROEMIO

Yo que sólo canté de la exquisita
partitura del íntimo decoro,
alzo hoy la voz a la mitad del foro
a la manera del tenor que imita
la gutural modulación del bajo,
para cortar a la epopeya un gajo.

Navegaré por las ondas civiles
con remos que no pesan, porque van
como los brazos del correo chuán
que remaba la Mancha con fusiles.

Diré con una épica sordina:
la patria es impecable y diamantina.

Suave Patria: permite que te envuelva
en la más honda música de selva
con que me modelaste todo entero
al golpe cadencioso de las hachas,
entre gritos y risas de muchachas
y pájaros de oficio carpintero.

Primer Acto

Patria: tu superficie es el maíz,
tus minas el palacio del Rey de Oros,
y tu cielo, las garzas en desliz
y el relámpago verde de los loros.

El Niño Dios te escrituró un establo
y los veneros de petróleo el diablo.

GENTLE FATHERLAND

PROEM

I who sang only from the exquisite
Score of intimate courtesy
Am raising my voice today, stage center,
In the manner of a tenor imitating
The guttural modulations of a bass,
To clip a twig from the epic poem.

I shall navigate upon civilian billows
With weightless oars, since they move
Like the arms of the Chuan courier*
Who used to row the English Channel with rifles.

I shall say in an epic, muted and minor,
The fatherland is diamantine and impeccable.

Gentle Fatherland: permit me to enfurl you
In the deepest music of the forest
With which you have modeled me completely
With the cadenced blows of hatchets,
Among loud cries and the laughter of girls
And birds of the woodpecking profession.

First Act

O Fatherland, the corn is your surface,
Your mines are the palace of the King of Coins,†
And your sky is the flying herons
And the green lightning of the parrots.

The Son of God has deeded you a stable
And the oil wells came from the devil.

---

* Jean Cottereau, called Jean Chuan, was the leader of a royalist insurrection in France in 1792. He was defeated by the republicans and took to guerrilla warfare. His partisans were called Chuans.

† Spanish playing cards employ the symbol of a golden coin instead of a heart. Hence the King of Coins is equivalent to the King of Hearts.

Sobre tu Capital, cada hora vuela
ojerosa y pintada, en carretela;
y en tu provincia, del reloj en vela
que rondan los palomos colipavos,
las campanadas caen como centavos.

Patria: tu mutilado territorio
se viste de percal y de abalorio.

Suave Patria: tu casa todavía
es tan grande, que el tren va por la vía
como aguinaldo de juguetería.

Y en el barullo de las estaciones,
con tu mirada de mestiza, pones
la inmensidad sobre los corazones.

¿Quién, en la noche que asusta a la rana,
no miró, antes de saber del vicio,
del brazo de su novia, la galana
pólvora de los juegos de artificio?

Suave Patria: en tu tórrido festín
luces policromías de delfín,
y con tu pelo rubio se desposa
el alma, equilibrista chuparrosa,
y a tus dos trenzas de tabaco, sabe
ofrendar aguamiel toda mi briosa
raza de bailadores de jarabe.

Tu barro suena a plata, y en tu puño,
su sonora miseria es alcancía;
y por las madrugadas del terruño,
en calles como espejos, se vacía
el santo olor de la panadería.

Over your capital each hour goes skimming
In a calash, heavy-eyed and painted;
And in your provinces, from the watchful clock
Around which the fantail pigeons are wheeling,
The strokes of the bell are falling like pennies.

Fatherland: your mutilated territory
Is dressed in glass beads and in calico.

Gentle Fatherland: your house is so huge,
Even yet, that the train travels along its track
Like a Christmas present in a toyshop.

And in the hubbub of the stations
With your mestizo's gaze you set
Immensity upon men's hearts.

In the night that fills the frogs with fear
Who has not seen, when innocent of evil,
With his sweetheart leaning on his arm,
The festive powder of fireworks?

Gentle Fatherland: In your torrid festival
You are lit up, many-colored as a dolphin,
And, an equilibrist humming bird,
With your golden skin the soul is married.
And with your two tobacco-colored tresses
You know how to offer maguey juice
To my spirited race of *jarabe* dancers.

Your clay sounds like silver and in your fist
Its sonorous poverty is an earthenware pig bank;
And at daybreak in small towns
There pours out, in streets like mirrors,
The blessed fragrance of the bakery.

Cuando nacemos, nos regalas notas,
después, un paraíso de compotas,
y luego te regalas toda entera,
suave Patria, alacena y pajarera.

Al triste y al feliz dices que sí,
que en tu lengua de amor prueben de tí
la picadura del ajonjolí.

¡Y tu cielo nupcial, que cuando truena
de deleites frenéticos nos llena!

Trueno de nuestras nubes, que nos baña
de locura, enloquece a la montaña,
requiebra a la mujer, sana al lunático,
incorpora a los muertos, pide el Viático,
y al fin derrumba las madererías
de Dios, sobre las tierras labrantías.

Trueno del temporal: oigo en tus quejas
crujir los esqueletos en parejas;
oigo lo que se fué, lo que aún no toco,
y la hora actual con su vientre de coco.
Y oigo en el brinco de tu ida y venida,
¡oh trueno, la ruleta de mi vida!

Intermedio

CUAUHTÉMOC
Joven abuelo: escúchame loarte,
único héroe a la altura del arte.

Anacrónicamente, absurdamente,
a tu nopal inclínase el rosal;
al idioma del blanco, tú lo imantas

When we are born, with music you regale us,
After that with a paradise of sweetmeats,
And then you give yourself to us wholly,
Gentle Fatherland, cupboard and aviary.

You acquiesce to both joy and sorrow
Which in your language of love taste of you
With the piquancy of sesame.

And your nuptial sky which, when it thunders,
Fills us with frantic pleasures!

Thunder from our clouds which bathes us
With madness, drives the mountain crazy,
Charms women, cures the lunatic,
Raises the dead, begs for the viaticum,
And finally tumbles the lumberyard of God
Upon the cultivated fields.

Thunderstorm, I hear in your muttering
Skeletons that go creaking in couples;
I hear what is past, what I do not yet touch,
And the present hour with its cocoanut belly.
And I hear in the skipping of your coming and going,
O thunder, the roulette wheel of my life.

Intermezzo

CUAUHTÉMOC*
Young ancestor: hear me praise you,
Single hero of artistic stature.

Anachronistically and absurdly,
To your cactus the rosebush inclines;
The white man's speech you magnetize

---

* Cuauhtémoc was the nephew and son-in-law of Moctezuma. He eventually succeeded to the Mexican throne and defended Mexico City bravely against the Spaniards. When the city fell he tried to escape in a canoe.

y es surtidor de católica fuente
que de responsos llena el victorial
zócalo de cenizas de tus plantas.

No como a César el rubor patricio
te cubre el rostro en medio del suplicio:
tu cabeza desnuda se nos queda
hemisféricamente, de moneda.

Moneda espiritual en que se fragua
todo lo que sufriste: la piragua
prisionera, el azoro de tus crías,
el sollozar de tus mitologías,
la Malinche, los ídolos a nado,
y por encima, haberte desatado
del pecho curvo de la emperatriz
como del pecho de una codorniz.

Segundo Acto

Suave Patria: tú vales por el río
de las virtudes de tu mujerío.
Tus hijas atraviesan como hadas,
o destilando un invisible alcohol,
vestidas con las redes de tu sol,
cruzan como botellas alambradas.

Suave Patria: te amo no cual mito,
sino por tu verdad de pan bendito,
como a niña que asoma por la reja
con la blusa corrida hasta la oreja
y la falda bajada hasta el huesito.

Inaccesible al deshonor, floreces;
creeré en tí, mientras una mexicana
en su tápalo lleve los dobleces
de la tienda, a las seis de la mañana,
y al estrenar su lujo, quede lleno
el país, del aroma del estreno.

And it is the jet from the Catholic spring
Filling with responses the triumphant
Pillar of ashes of your plants.

Not like Caesar does patrician modesty
Veil your face in the midst of torture;
Your naked head is with us still
Hemispherically on our money.

Spiritual coin in which is smelted
All that you suffered, the captured canoe
And the bewilderment of your children,
The sobbing of your mythologies,
La Malinche,* the floating idols,
And the climax, how you were torn away
From the rounded breast of the empress
As from the breast of a mother quail.

Second Act

Gentle Fatherland: you are worth the river
Of virtues of your womanhood.
Your daughters pass like fairies
Or distilling an invisible alcohol,
Dressed in the nets of your sunshine,
They walk abroad like netted bottles.

Gentle Fatherland: I love you not as a legend
But for the truth of your blessed bread,
As I love a girl appearing at the grillwork
With her blouse reaching to her ears
And her skirt down to her ankles.

Inaccessible to dishonor, you flourish;
I shall believe in you while a Mexican woman,
Dressed in her best at six in the morning,
Wears a shawl still creased from the store
And leaves the land overflowing
With the fragrance of her first appearance.

* The Indian mistress of Cortez.

Como la sota moza, Patria mía,
en piso de metal, vives al día,
de milagro, como la lotería.

Tu imagen, el Palacio Nacional,
con tu misma grandeza y con tu igual
estatura de niño y de dedal.

Te dará, frente al hambre y el obús,
un higo San Felipe de Jesús.

Suave Patria, vendedora de chía:
quiero raptarte en la cuaresma opaca,
sobre un garañón, y con matraca,
y entre los tiros de la policía.

Tus entrañas no niegan un asilo
para el ave que el párvulo sepulta
en una caja de carretes de hilo,
y nuestra juventud, llorando, oculta
dentro de tí, el cadáver hecho poma
de aves que hablan nuestro mismo idioma.

Si me ahogo en tus julios, a mí baja
desde el vergel de tu peinado denso,
frescura de rebozo y de tinaja:
y si tirito, dejas que me arrope
en tu respiración azul de incienso
y en tus carnosos labios de rompope.

Por tu balcón de palmas bendecidas
el Domingo de Ramos, yo desfilo
lleno de sombra, porque tú trepidas.

Like a young card damsel †, O my country,
On a metal floor, you live for the day
Of miracles, like the lottery.

Your image, the National Palace,
With your same greatness and your same childish
And Tom Thumb stature.

Faced with hunger and with shrapnel,
San Felipe de Jesús will give you a fig.

Gentle Fatherland, vendor of sage:
I should like to abduct you in the Lenten fiesta,
Riding on a stallion, with a rattle
Among the shots of the policemen.

Your soul does not deny asylum
To the bird the little boy buries
In a box for spools of thread,
And our boyhood, weeping, hides within you
The body, transformed into apple,
Of birds that speak our own language.

If you stifle me in your Julys, you lower to me
From the garden of your thick coiffure
The coolness of shawl and earthenware;
And if I shiver, you let me wrap myself
In your breath, blue with incense,
In your fleshy lips of *rompope.**

By your balcony of blessed palms
On Palm Sunday I pass full of shadow
Because you are trembling.

† The sota or jack of the Spanish playing cards is a female figure.
* *Rompope* is an eggnog made with rum.

Quieren morir tu ánima y tu estilo,
cual muriéndose van las cantadoras
que en las ferias, con el bravío pecho
empitonando la camisa, han hecho
la lujuria y el ritmo de las horas.

Patria, te doy de tu dicha la clave:
sé siempre igual, fiel a tu espejo diario;
cincuenta veces es igual el Ave
taladrada en el hilo de rosario,
y es más feliz que tú, Patria suave.

Sé igual y fiel; pupilas de abandono;
sedienta voz, la trigarante faja
en tus pechugas al vapor; y un trono
a la intemperie, cual una sonaja:
la carreta alegórica de paja!

El són del corazón

Your spirit and your grace seek to die
As the singing women go toward death
Who, in the fairs, with rugged breasts
Goring their blouses, have made
The rhythm and the lewdness of the hours.

Fatherland, I give you the key to all your joy:
Be always the same, faithful to your daily mirror;
The Ave, fifty times the same,
Is strung upon the thread of the rosary
And is happier than you, Gentle Fatherland.

Be the same and faithful; with languid pupils;
Thirsty voice, the tricolored sash†
Over your bare bosom; and a throne outdoors,
Happy as a lark:
The allegorical wagon of straw!

† A reference to the Mexican flag, introduced by the Emperor Iturbide in
1821, its colors symbolizing unity, peace, and independence.

LUIS CARLOS LOPEZ
(de Escuariza)

b. 1883, Cartagena, Colombia

LUIS CARLOS LOPEZ
(de Escuariza)

b. 1883, Cartagena, Colombia

L C. LOPEZ is at the present time Colombian consul
in Baltimore. His work represents the culmination
of the naturalistic trend in the postmodernist move-
ment, a revolt against sweet musicality and introspective
aestheticism. No subject is too prosaic or too vulgar for his
sardonic verses. Technically he is also a revolutionary, for
though he often writes in the sonnet form, his rhythms are
halting and intentionally harsh. An unsparing critic of the
boredom and sterility of provincial life, his sharpest barbs
are aimed at small-town bourgeoisie whom he sees as orang-
utangs in sandals or as piggish gluttons. For the priest, the
local official, or the politician he has nothing but contempt.
Although López has been criticized as unpoetic, he has had
a tremendous influence throughout Spanish America. The
number of his imitators proves how typical of all the repub-
lics are the genre scenes which he sketches so vividly. His
attitude is a negative one and somewhat reactionary; al-
though he despises his environment he has nothing to put
in its place except a hankering for the good old days. What
gives his poetry its peculiar force and sets him apart from
the other realistic postmodernists is his unrestrained brutal-
ity, his bitter sense of humor which is almost reminiscent of
Swift. López perfected his method at the very beginning of
his career and his subsequent books show no change or de-
velopment. He has gradually come to be recognized as su-
preme in his particular field of satire.

Among the poems which follow, "A mi ciudad nativa" is

noteworthy for a certain sentimentality, proof that, for all his assumed toughness, López has secretly a good deal in common with the melancholy modernists. The comparison of the sun to a fried egg in "Despilfarros IV" is typical of the kind of humorous imagery which López introduced into Spanish American poetry.

De mi villorrio. Madrid, 1908.
Posturas difíciles. ? 1909.
Varios a varios (collaboration with M. Cervera and E. López). ? 1910.
Por el atajo. Cartagena, 1928.

EL ALCALDE

El Alcalde, de sucio jipijapa de copa,
ceñido de una banda de seda tricolor,
panzudo a lo Capeto, muy holgada la ropa,
luce por el poblacho su perfil de bull-dog.

Hombre de pelo en pecho, rubio como la estopa,
rubrica con la punta de su machete, y por
la noche cuando toma la lugareña sopa
de tallarines y ajos, se afloja el cinturón.

Su mujer, una chica nerviosamente guapa,
que lo tiene cogido como con una grapa,
gusta de las grasientas obras de Paul de Kock,

ama los abalorios y se pinta las cejas,
mientras que su consorte luce por las callejas
su barriga, mil dijes y una cara feroz.

De mi villorrio (1908)

THE MAYOR

The mayor in a dirty, high-crowned panama,
Girdled with a silken tricolor sash,
Big-bellied as Hugh Capet, his clothes worn very loose,
Displays his bulldog profile through the village.

A man with hair on his chest, towheaded,
Who signs his name with the point of his machete
And, when at night he drinks his local soup
With noodles and garlic, lets his belt out.

His wife, a pretty, high-strung girl,
Has got her hooks in him.
She enjoys the greasy works of Paul de Koch,

She likes glass beads and uses eyebrow pencil
While her consort is wearing through the alleys,
His paunch, his myriad watch charms, and a tough look.

MUCHACHAS SOLTERANAS

> Susana ven; tu amor
> quiero gozar.
> > Lehar opereta, "La Casta Susana."

Muchachas solteras de provincia
que los años hilvanan
leyendo folletines
y atisbando en balcones y ventanas . . .

Muchachas de provincia,
las de aguja y dedal, que no hacen nada
sin tomar de noche
café con leche y dulce de papaya . . .

Muchachas de provincia,
que salen—si es que salen de la casa—
muy temprano a la iglesia,
con un andar doméstico de gansas.

Muchachas de provincia,
papandujas, etcétera, que cantan
melancólicamente
de sol a sol;—Susana, ven . . . Susana . . .

Pobres muchachas, pobres
muchachas tan inútiles y castas,
que hacen decir al diablo,
con los brazos en cruz;—Pobres muchachas!—

Biblioteca Aldeana de Colombia, Vol. 85

OLD MAIDS

"Come Susanna: I want
to enjoy your love."
Lehar operetta, *The Chaste Susanna.*

Provincial old maids
Sewed up by the years,
Reading love-story magazines
And peering into balconies and windows . . .

Provincial old maids,
They of the needle and thimble who do nothing
Except consume each night
Café-au-lait and papaya sweetmeats . . .

Provincial old maids,
Who go out—if they do leave the house—
Very early on their way to church,
Walking with the domesticated waddle of a goose.

Provincial old maids,
Overripe, et cetera, who sing
In a melancholy way
From sun to sun:—Susanna, come . . . Susanna . . .

Poor old maids, poor
Old maids so useless and so chaste,
Who make the devil say
With folded arms:—Poor old maids!—

A MI CIUDAD NATIVA

("Ciudad triste, ayer reina
de la mar." J. M. de Heredia.)

Noble rincón de mis abuelos: nada
como evocar, cruzando callejuelas,
los tiempos de la cruz y de la espada,
del ahumado candil y las pajuelas . . .

Pues ya pasó, ciudad amurallada,
tu edad de folletín . . . Las carabelas
se fueron para siempre de tu rada . . .
—Ya no viene el aceite en botijuelas!

Fuiste heroica en los años coloniales,
cuando tus hijos, águilas caudales,
no eran una caterva de vencejos.

Mas hoy, plena de rancio desaliño,
bien puedes inspirar ese cariño
que uno le tiene a sus zapatos viejos . . .

Por el atajo (1928)

DESPILFARROS

I V

Desde mi cuarto miro la plazuela,
donde corren los chicos
que salen de la escuela
municipal.

Con vuelo de pericos
la estudiantil parvada
se aleja, entre los rotos abanicos
de los árboles . . .

TO MY NATIVE CITY

"Sad city, formerly queen of the sea."
J. M. de Heredia.

Noble spot of my ancestors: there's nothing
Like evoking, when walking through the alleys,
The ages of the cross and broadsword,
Smoky oil lamps and straws tipped with sulphur* . . .

For it's all over, O walled city, finished
With your sword-and-cloak romance . . . the galleons
Are gone forever from your harbor . . .
Even olive oil doesn't come in earthenware!

You were so heroic in colonial years
When your sons were golden eagles,
Not a gang of wretched sparrows.

But today, a rancid sloven,
You can still inspire that same affection
A man has for a worn out pair of shoes.

RUBBISH

IV

From my room I look upon the little plaza
Where the kids go running
As they come out of the
Public school.

Flying like parakeets,
The rabble of students
Moves off under the broken
Fans of the trees.

* Straws tipped with sulphur were ancestors of the match.

Nada
turba el largo silencio. Y solamente
repite el mismo tema
de la fuente,
la oquedad del ambiente
solitario,
mientras el sol, como una enorme yema
de huevo frito, atisba tristemente
sobre la cruz de un campanario . . .

V I I

La sombra que proyecta mi aposento
dibuja en un tejado
y una pared la oreja de un jumento
y una sartén . . .

La oreja
se alarga en el crepúsculo morado
dando la sensación
del caminar de una pantufla vieja,
y la sartén se mete en un balcón . . .

¿No es un presentimiento
matrimonial? . . . Y, como un argumento,
se oye una tremolina
que invade la quietud de mi aposento . . .
¡Y es que un gallo persigue a una gallina!

Por el atajo

                              Nothing
Ruffles the long silence. And only
The same theme of the fountain
Is repeated
By the vacancy of the solitary
Ambient air,
While the sun like an enormous
Yoke of fried egg peers sadly
Over the cross on top of a belfry.

                    V I I

The shadow which my bedroom throws
Sketches on a roof
And on a wall an ass's ear
And a frying pan . . .

                              The ear
Grows longer in the purple twilight,
Giving the impression
Of an old slipper walking
And the frying pan intrudes upon a balcony . . .

Is not this a matrimonial
Presentiment? . . . And like a demonstration,
An audible disturbance
Invades my bedroom's quietude . . .
And it's a hen being run down by a rooster!

A UN PERRO

¡Ah, perro miserable,
que aún vives del cajón de la bazofia,
—como cualquier político—temiendo
las sorpresas del palo de la escoba!

¡Y provocando siempre
que hurtas en el cajón pleno de sobras,
—como cualquier político—la triste
protesta estomacal de ávidas moscas!

Para después ladrarle
por las noches, bien harto de carroña,
—como cualquier político—a la luna
creyendo que es algún queso de bola . . .

¡Ah perro miserable,
que humilde ocultas con temor la cola,
—como cualquier político del día—
¡¡y no te da un ataque de hidrofobia!!

Por el atajo

A SATAN

Satán,

te pido un alma sencilla y complicada
como la tuya. Un alma feliz en su dolor.
tú gozas—y yo envidio tu alegre carcajada—
si un tigre, por ejemplo, se come a un ruiseñor.

TO A DOG

O wretched dog,
Still living off the garbage can—
Like some politician—and afraid of
The surprises of the broomstick!

Ever stirring up
By what you steal out of the refuse can—
Like some politician—the sad
Belly protest of the avid flies!

To go on barking afterward
At night, well stuffed with carrion—
Like some politician—at the moon,
Believing it to be a lump of cheese . . .

O wretched dog,
You meekly hide your tail in fear—
Like some current politician—
Watch out you don't get hydrophobia!

TO SATAN

Oh, grant me, Satan, a soul simple and complex
Even as yours is. A soul happy in its torment.
You are joyful—and I envy you your gay guffaws—
When a tiger, for example, eats up a nightingale.

¡Mi vida, esta mi vida te ofrece una trastada! . . .
—Mi vida, flor inútil, sin tallo y sin olor,
se dobla mustiamente ya casi deshojada . . .
Y el tedio es un gusano peludo en esa flor.

¡Pensar diez disparates y hacer mil disparates! . . .
Pues tú, Satán, no ignoras que yo perdí el camino,
y es triste—aquí en la tierra del coco y del café—

vivir como las cosas en los escaparates,
para de un aneurisma morir cual mi vecino . . .
—Murió sentado en eso que llaman W.C.!

Por el atajo

My life, this life of mine, offers you its folly! . . .
My life, a useless flower, without perfume, without a stem,
Bends languidly and very nearly leafless . . .
And boredom is a hairy worm within this blossom.

To think of ten blunders and make a thousand blunders! . . .
But you, O Satan, know that I have lost the road.
And it is sad—here in this land of cocoanuts and coffee—

To live like the wares shut up in showcases,
Only to die of an aneurysm, just as my neighbor
Died—seated in what is called the W. C.!

VICENTE HUIDOBRO

b. 1893, Santiago de Chile

VICENTE HUIDOBRO

b. 1893, Santiago de Chile

HUIDOBRO introduced European experimental writing into Chilean literature. A descendant of the Spanish aristocracy of Chile, he went to Europe at the age of twenty-four to continue his literary studies. His first two books of poetry were symbolist in tone but in Paris, in 1918, he began publishing with the cubists. At this time he was arranging poems in pictorial shapes in the manner of Guillaume Apollinaire. In 1921 he actually had an exhibition of poems in a picture gallery. He also visited Madrid while ultraism still flourished, and eventually launched his own movement, creationism. There has been much controversy over the actual origin of creationism and the poet's debt to his French contemporaries. He himself says his theories were formulated as early as 1916. They emphasize the conscious creation of new images. "The poet creates the world that ought to exist outside of the one that does exist . . . The poet is concerned with expressing only the inexpressible." Poetry for Huidobro is a kind of musical pattern of images, an international language independent of any specific language. In consequence much of his work is written in French. He is said to have influenced Juan Larrea and Gerardo Diego of Spain and Pablo de Rokha and Angel Cruchaga of Chile. Several members of the most recent generation of Chilean poets also owe something to his innovations. Huidobro is active as well as a novelist and playwright. His work is extremely literary, elegant in design, and remarkable for humorous verbal legerdemain. Conservative critics disparage its value. They cannot forgive him for the picture poems, his disregard for punctuation, and his fantastic imagery. He is important, however, as a pioneer of the vanguardist movement in both French and Spanish literature and his poetry has undeniable charm.

The poem, "Emigrante a América," has been included as a sample of his early writing in a somewhat ultraist vein. "Preludio de esperanza," despite its modern images, is thoroughly romantic and indicates how much of the symbolist mood still lingers in the work of a poet who is considered an ultra-radical. "Ronda de la vida riendo" is especially interesting for the emergence of a social theme. The repetitive technique used in this poem and also in "En" is similar to the method of Gertrude Stein.

Canciones en la noche. Santiago de Chile, 1913.
La gruta del silencio. Santiago de Chile, 1913.
Espejo de agua. Buenos Aires, 1916.
Hallali. Madrid, 1918.
Ecuatorial. Madrid, 1918.
Cagliostro (novel). Madrid, 1918.
Poemas árticos. Madrid, 1918.
Saisons choisies. Paris, 1921.
Manifestes (essays). Paris, 1925.
Vientos contrarios (essays). Santiago de Chile, 1926.
Mío Cid campeador (novel). Madrid, 1929; 2nd ed. Santiago de Chile, 1942.
Temblor de cielo. Madrid, 1931; 2nd ed. Santiago de Chile, 1942.
Altazor. Madrid, 1931.
Gilles de Raiz (play). Paris, 1932.
En la luna (play). Santiago de Chile, 1934.
Sátiro (novel). Santiago de Chile, 1938.
El ciudadano del olvido. Santiago de Chile, 1941.
Ver y palpar. Santiago de Chile, 1941.

EMIGRANTE A AMERICA

Estrellas eléctricas
Se encienden en el viento

> Y algunos signos astrológicos
> Han caído al mar

> Ese emigrante que canta
> Partirá mañana

Vivir

> Buscar

Atado al barco

> Como un horóscopo
Veinte días sobre el mar

Bajo las aguas
Nadan los pulpos vegetales

Detrás del horizonte
> El otro puerto

Entre el boscaje
Las rosas deshojadas
> Iluminan las calles

Poemas árticos (1918)

EMIGRANT TO AMERICA

Electric stars
Burn in the wind

And certain astrological signs
Have fallen into the sea

This emigrant that sings
Will set out tomorrow

To live

To seek

Tied up to the ship

Like a horoscope
Twenty days on the sea

Beneath the waters
Swim vegetable octopuses

Beyond the horizon
The other harbor

Among the bushes
Roses without leaves

Illuminate the streets

PRELUDIO DE ESPERANZA

Cantas y cantas hablas y hablas
Y ruedas por el tiempo
Y lloras como lirio desatado
Y suspiras entre largos agonizantes que no saben qué decir
A veces también ríes con tus huesos de gran noche
Señalados en su sitio de esqueleto
Designados en su trozo de tierra saludando al cielo
Pide conformidad para tus altos intereses
En el país de la esperanza que despierta en tus costillas
Pide lección al árbol acusado por sus excesos
Y sus alas habituadas a todo trance
Escucha la salida del río escucha la sombra adentro de la flor

Cantas y cantas hablas y hablas
Y sueñas que la especie olvidará tinieblas
Pronto pronto el olvido del llanto
Las lágrimas armadas de tan lejana luz
Como animales numerados que van saliendo del mar
Pronto el olvido de tanta sombra suspirada
Pronto el futuro de horizontes que conoce su pasión

Cantas y cantas
Y tienes una voz acumulada
Tienes una voz con ciertos lados dolorosos
Y ciertos rincones impacientes
Y gotas de astros perdidos por su tierno corazón
Tienes cascadas en tus regiones más pensadoras
Tienes objetos convertidos en vidrio al fondo de tus ojos
Tienes rutas nacidas para el oscuro sonar de la garganta
Puedes hacer un nudo de puertas con tus enigmas
Y así mismo desatar el tiempo entre sonidos y presagios
Puedes dar una parte a tu luz en el camino mismo

PRELUDE TO HOPE

You sing and sing you talk and talk
As you roll through time
And you weep like a detached lily
And you sigh between long periods of dying that do not
    know what to say
At times you laugh too with your bones of deep night
Emphasized in their skeletal position
Designated in their fragment of earth greeting the sky
Seek for agreement with your chief interests
In the country of hope that opens in your ribs
Seek a lesson in the tree indicated by its excesses
And its wings accustomed to any emergency
Listen to the departure of the river listen to the shadow
    within the flower

You sing and sing you talk and talk
And you dream that the species shall forget darkness
Soon soon the forgetfulness of weeping
Tears armed with such distant light
Like numbered animals emerging from the sea
Soon the forgetfulness of so much sighed-for shadow
Soon the future of horizons that knows its passion

You sing and sing
And you have an accumulated voice
You have a voice with certain sad sides
And certain impatient corners
And drops of stars lost through its tender heart
You have cascades in your most thoughtful regions
You have objects changed into glass in the depths of your
    eyes
You have highways born for the secret sound of the throat
You can tie a knot of doors with your enigmas
And likewise untie time between noises and omens
You can make a place for your light in the same road

Hablas y hablas
Y ya sabemos que es como el ruido de la lluvia
Que cae de cabeza sobre el campo
Pero tu ruido lleva sueños y puntas de hojas pensativas
Lleva un bronce que ha escarbado cenizas y montañas

Cantas y cantas lloras y lloras
Y en tu llorar hay el combate de la muerte y de la marcha
Todas las últimas batallas con su color de límite
Y en tu silencio crecen árboles tan decididos como las borras-
    cas
Y la muerte obedece a su mundo tembloroso
Ardiendo en sueños de clave visionaria

Hablas y hablas miras y miras
Y sientes la corteza que te separa de las ansias ajenas
Sientes desde adentro de ti mismo
Los impulsos del mundo los latidos de la tierra
Y los tormentos de todas las crisálidas
En su escafandra de enigmas
Sientes las alas ciegas de tus signos jadeantes
Y esa agua olvidada de sus mares que corre en tus arterias

Cantas y cantas ríes y ríes
Y tienes una dulzura que te come los huesos
Y oyes crujir la tierra que no sabe su nombre
Y le duelen los árboles
Le duele el mar con todas sus olas
Le duele el paso de los hombres
Y los arroyos oscuros que se entrecruzan
En un pacto ungido por la nobleza de sus años

Lloras y lloras miras y miras ríes y ríes
Y te detienes pensativo en medio de tantos ecos
En esta tierra de entusiasmos secretos
En estos vientos que traen apariencias de destinos
Y contemplas de un lado el empezar del mundo

You talk and talk
And already we know it is like the sound of rain
Which falls headlong over the field
But your sound bears dreams and tips of pensive leaves
It bears a bronze that has scoured ashes and mountains

You sing and sing you weep and weep
And in your weeping there is the battle of death and progress
All the ultimate battles with their boundary color
And trees grow in your silence as determined as tempests
And death obeys its trembling world
Burning in dreams of visionary cipher

You talk and talk you look and look
And you feel the rind that separates you from distant desires
You feel from within yourself
The impulses of the world the throbbing of the earth
And the torments of all chrysalises
In their diving suit of enigmas
You feel the blind wings of your palpitating signals
And that forgotten water of their seas that flows in your
      arteries

You sing and sing you laugh and laugh
And you have a sweetness that eats up your bones
And you hear the earth cracking that does not know its own
      name
And the trees hurt it
And the sea with all its waves hurts it
The footsteps of men hurt it
And secret intersecting rivulets
And a covenant consecrated by the nobility of its years

You weep and weep you look and look you laugh and laugh
And you pause pensively in the midst of so many echoes
In this earth of secret enthusiasms
In these winds that carry appearances of destinies
And on one hand you contemplate the beginning of the world

Del otro la noche de vidrios espantados
Y te vas y buscas ansioso
Esa música rasgada por donde se evade la casa
Y desaparece moviendo el corazón entre fantasmas
Cuando el sol te reemplaza de repente
Qué quieres que te diga
A tiempo de mirar caen las plumas
Como vejez de palabra en traje de alma
Qué quieres que te diga
El mundo baja por tus angustias a tu encuentro

Cantas y cantas hablas y hablas
Y te olvidas de todo para que todo te olvide
Hablas y hablas cantas y cantas
Lloras y lloras miras y miras ríes y ríes
Y te vas en silueta de aire

El ciudadano del olvido (1941)

TIEMPO DE ESPERA

Pasan los días
La eternidad no llega ni el milagro

Pasan los días
El barco no se acerca
El mar no se hace flor ni campanario
No se descubre la caída

Pasan los días
Las piedras lloran con sus huesos azules
Pero no se abre la puerta
No se descubre la caída de la noche
Ni la ciencia en su cristal
Ni el comprender ni la apariencia ni la hojarasca del porqué

Pasan los días
No sale adolescencia
Ni atmósfera vivida ni misterio

And on the other the night of frightened windowpanes
And you go and anxiously seek
That torn music through which the house escapes
And the heart disappears moving among fantoms
When the sun suddenly supersedes you
What do you want me to say to you
While we look at them feathers fall
Like worn-out words in the dress of the soul
What do you want me to say to you
The world descends through your afflictions to meet you

You sing and sing you talk and talk
And you forget everything so that everything may forget you
You talk and talk you sing and sing
You weep and weep you look and look you laugh and laugh
And you go silhouetted in air

TIME OF WAITING

The days go by
Eternity does not come nor the miracle

The days go by
The ship does not approach
The sea does not turn into flower or belfry
The fall is not revealed

The days go by
Stones weep with their blue bones
But the door does not open
The fall of night is not revealed
Nor science in its crystal
Nor the understanding nor the appearance nor the dead
    leaves of why

The days go by
Adolescence does not emerge
Nor living atmosphere nor mystery

Pasan los días
El ojo no se hace mundo
Las tristezas no se hacen pensamiento
El mar no llega hasta mis pies agonizando

Pasan los días
Y ella es pulmón de noches rompiéndose en sonidos
Y es hermosa como llanura comprendida
Es abundancia de sauces y silencios

Pasan los días
Ella es huracán que desata sus ruidos
Es una gran lágrima cayendo interminablemente
Como una estrella que se volviera loca

Pasan los días
El miraje infinito de las tumbas una a una
No detiene la marcha
Se abren paso hacia el día hacia las horas
Hacia la edad y sus malezas

Pasan los días
Y no se oye el ruido de la luna

El ciudadano del olvido

NATURALEZA VIVA

Él deja al acordeón el fin del mundo
Paga con la lluvia la última canción
Allí donde las voces se juntan nace un enorme cedro
Más confortable que el cielo

Una golondrina me dice papá
Una anemona me dice mamá

Azul azul allí y en la boca del lobo
Azul Señor Cielo que se aleja
Qué dice usted é Hacia dónde irá

The days go by
The eye does not turn into the world
Sorrows do not turn into ideas
The sea does not come dying to my feet

The days go by
And she is the lung of the nights breaking into sounds
And beautiful as smoothness embraced
She is abundance of willows and silences

The days go by
She is a hurricane unloosing its noises
She is a great tear interminably falling
Like a star that is going mad

The days go by
The infinite mirage of tombs one after another
Does not hinder progress
They open softly to the day to the hours
Toward the age and its weeds

The days go by
And the sound of the moon is not heard

NATURE VIVE

He leaves the end of the world to the accordion
Pays for the last song with rain
Yonder where the voices unite an enormous cedar is born
More comfortable than the sky

A swallow says to me papa
An anemone says to me mama

Blue blue over yonder and in the mouth of the wolf
Mr. Blue Sky departing
What do you say Where will you go

Ah el hermoso brazo azul azul
Dad el brazo a la Señora Nube
Si tenéis miedo del lobo
El lobo de la boca azul azul
Del diente largo largo
Para devorar a la abuela naturaleza

Señor Cielo rasque su golondrina
Señora Nube apague sus anemonas

Las voces se juntan sobre el pájaro
Más grande que el árbol de la creación
Más hermoso que una corriente de aire entre dos astros

Ver y palpar (1941)

E N

El corazón del pájaro
El corazón que brilla en el pájaro
El corazón de la noche
La noche del pájaro
El pájaro del corazón de la noche

Si la noche cantara en el pájaro
En el pájaro olvidado en el cielo
El cielo perdido en la noche
Te diría lo que hay en el corazón que brilla en el pájaro

La noche perdida en el cielo
El cielo perdido en el pájaro
El pájaro perdido en el olvido del pájaro
La noche perdida en la noche
El cielo perdido en el cielo

Pero el corazón es el corazón del corazón
Y habla por la boca del corazón

Ver y palpar

Ah what a beautiful blue blue arm
Give your arm to Mrs. Cloud
If you're afraid of the wolf
The wolf with the blue blue mouth
With long long teeth
To eat up grandmother nature

Mr. Sky scrape off your swallow
Mrs. Cloud put out your anemone

The voices unite over the bird
Larger than the tree of creation
Lovelier than a current of air between two stars

I N

The heart of the bird
The heart that shines in the bird
The heart of the night
The night of the bird
The bird of the heart of the night

If the night should sing in the bird
In the bird forgotten in the sky
The sky lost in the night
I should say what there is in the heart that shines in the bird

The night lost in the sky
The sky lost in the bird
The bird lost in the oblivion of the bird
The night lost in the night
The sky lost in the sky

But the heart is the heart of the heart
And speaks with the mouth of the heart

RONDA DE LA
VIDA RIENDO

I

Trescientos sesenta y cinco árboles tiene la selva
Trescientas sesenta y cinco selvas tiene el año
Cuántas se necesitan para formar un siglo
Un niño se perdería en ellas hasta el fin del siglo
Y aprendería el canto de todos los pájaros

Los árboles doblan la cabeza cuando los niños lanzan piedras
Las piedras en el aire saludan a los pájaros y piden una
     canción
Una canción con los ojos azules
Una canción con los cabellos largos
Una canción dividida como una naranja
Con una historia adentro llena de sonrisas o si usted prefiere
     llena de lágrimas
Las lágrimas agitan las manos antes de ahogarse
Y las sonrisas saludan a las gentes desde lejos como las
     piedras
Buenos días y Hasta luego son los hijos de la boca que va a
     enamorarse pronto
El sol también dice buenos días cuando los árboles aletean
Y dice hasta luego cuando la montaña cierra los ojos
Hasta luego entre las olas aceitadas del mar
Hasta luego diría yo también porque ahora el cielo trae una
     bandeja llena de flores
Así es agradable la vida como un jugo de naranja lleno de
     historias de niños entre los dientes de las niñas
Así es fresca la vida y puede correr como los perros entre
     los colores sueltos
O como los ríos que seguían a los abuelos

Las flores hacen gracias al borde del camino
Los árboles balbucean a nuestros ojos cosas tan claras que
     es imposible no comprender

SERENADE OF LAUGHING LIFE

I

The forest has three hundred and sixty-five trees
The year has three hundred and sixty-five forests
How many does it take to make up a century
A child would be lost in them up to the end of the century
And would learn all the bird songs

The trees bend their heads when children throw stones at
    them
Stones in the air greet the birds and ask for a song
A song with blue eyes
A song with long hair
A song divided like an orange
With a story inside full of smiles or if you prefer it full of
    tears
And the tears wave their hands before choking themselves
And the smiles greet people from afar like the stones
Good Day and Good-By are sons of the mouth that will soon
    fall in love
The sun says good-by too when the trees move their wings
And it says good-by when the mountain closes its eyes
Good-by among the oily waves of the sea
I would say good-by too because the sky now brings a tray-
    ful of flowers
So life is pleasant as orange juice full of children's stories be-
    tween the teeth of little girls
So life is cool and can run like dogs among loosened colors
Or like rivers that used to follow our grandfathers

Flowers play pranks alongside the road
The trees babble directly in front of us things so clear that
    we cannot misunderstand them

Los árboles tienen quince años y las flores dan sus primeros
    pasos
Los árboles dicen buenos días y esperan que el sol se anude
    la corbata y se ponga el sombrero

Así es agradable la vida
La vida con su velocidad aterradora
La vida con trescientos sesenta y cinco árboles para escalar
    alegremente
La vida con sus flores como corbatas
La vida con sus mugidos trepando por la tarde
Lentos como los ojos de la tarde
El sol dice buenas noches y se va hasta que los árboles vuel-
    van a ocupar su sitio religiosamente

Así sería agradable la vida
Pero los hombres se miran con ojos de fogata
Se buscan en los rincones con dedos de puñales
Se buscan entre los árboles dormidos para hacerse esclavos
Entonces maldecimos la vida y empuñamos las manos
Entonces gritamos en las noches a la montaña
Viva la muerte con su velocidad aterradora
Con su velocidad que no enmohece nunca

I I

Trescientos sesenta y cinco dedos tiene el árbol
Trescientas sesenta y cinco manos tienen los ojos azules
Lo mismo los ojos negros
Lo mismo los cabellos largos
Y las naranjas y las orejas que ruedan a través del siglo
Trescientos sesenta y cinco cantos tiene la garganta
Lo mismo las olas pedregosas del mar
Lo mismo las piedras aceitadas en el aire
Lo mismo la bandeja del cielo
Y el sol que dice buenas noches y cierra la puerta

The trees are fifteen years old and the flowers are just begin-
ning to walk
The trees say good day and wait until the sun knots its tie
and puts on its hat

So life is pleasant
Life with its terrifying speed
Life with its three hundred and sixty-five trees to be joyfully
climbed
Life with its flowers like neckties
Life with its bellowing that mounts through the evening
Slow as the eyes of the evening
The sun says good night and goes away until the trees return
religiously to take their places

So life would be pleasant
But men look at each other with blazing eyes
Seek each other in corners with daggers for fingers
Seek each other among the sleeping trees to make slaves of
each other
Then we curse life and clench our fists
Then we cry out at night to the mountain
death with its terrifying speed
With its speed that never gets rusty

I I

The tree has three hundred and sixty-five fingers
The blue eyes have three hundred and sixty-five hands
The same for black eyes
The same for long hair
And the oranges and the ears that roll across the century
The throat has three hundred and sixty-five songs
The same for the stony waves of the sea
The same for the oily stones in the air
The same for the tray of the sky
And the sun that says good night and closes the door

Los bigotes del árbol encanecen rápidamente
Y se agitan al ritmo de su risa y de las risas de los niños
Los árboles tienen ochenta años y las risas dan los primeros
    pasos
Las lágrimas caen por el tronco del árbol
Las risas trepan por el cielo
Adentro del corazón se abre una naranja llena de luces y de
    colores
Los colores trepan por las ramas del árbol
Y trepan por los cabellos largos
Y se pasean al fondo de los ojos azules
O se pierden al fondo de los ojos negros

Buenos días y Hasta luego están parados al principio y al fin
    de cada historia
Y la historia está llena de árboles de niños de piedras y de
    olas
Los nietos dicen buenos días
Los abuelos dicen hasta luego
Los árboles crecen como los cabellos
Las olas brillan como los ojos azules
Los pájaros ríen como los ojos negros

Así es agradable la vida y puede cantar como las flores
Así es fresca la vida y puede reír como los ríos
La vida con su velocidad aterradora
La vida con sus árboles
Con sus sombreros
Con sus corbatas
Con sus ojos azules trepando por el cielo
Con sus cabellos largos cayendo por la tierra
La vida con el mugido de sus árboles en la tarde
La vida con sus piedras y sus olas enmohecidas
Con sus ríos que pasan mirando a todo el mundo
Con sus pájaros que aplauden las canciones
Así sería agradable la vida
Pero hay aún muchos fantasmas que se pasean por la vida
Fabricantes de mártires para cubrir el canto de las olas
    espiando que la presa se distraiga

The tree's moustache grows rapidly gray
And waves to the rhythm of its laughter and the laughter of
   children
The trees are eighty years old and the laughter is just begin-
   ning to walk
Tears fall along the trunk of the tree
Laughter mounts through the sky
An orange full of lights and colors opens within the heart
Colors mount through the branches of the tree
And mount through long hair
And take a walk into the depths of blue eyes
Or get lost in the depths of black eyes

Good Day and Good-By are drawn up at the beginning and
   the end of each story
And the story is full of trees children stones and waves
Grandchildren say good day
Grandfathers say good-by
The trees grow like hair
The waves shine like blue eyes
The birds laugh like black eyes

So life is pleasant and can sing like the flowers
So life is cool and can laugh like the rivers
Life with its terrifying speed
Life with its trees
With its hats
With its neckties
With its blue eyes mounting through the sky
With its long hair falling through the earth
Life with the bellowing of its trees in the evening
Life with its stones and its rusty waves
With its rivers that pass by looking at all the world
With its birds applauding the songs
And so life would be pleasant
But there are fantoms too that walk through life
Makers of martyrs to cover the songs of the waves
             lying in wait until the prey is heedless

Ellos se pasean con las manos en los bolsillos
Con la arrogancia en el hueco del sombrero
Y un látigo en cada ojo
Se pasean en sus zapatos luminosos como ataúdes
Se pasean como ataúdes en sus ataúdes

Esos espectros viven de la sangre de millones de hombres
Y porque ellos viven en la vida la vida es detestable
Y los hombres prefieren la muerte
La muerte con su marcha que no enmohece nunca

I I I

Trescientos sesenta y cinco pájaros tiene el cielo
Estos pájaros serán banderas el día del gran triunfo
Cuando los hombres oigan cantar la hora del hombre
Cuando nadie viva del esfuerzo nacido en otros pechos
Cuando nadie se nutra de la carne ajena
Ni respire por pulmones extraños
Ni se ate los pantalones con las tripas esclavas

Trescientos sesenta y cinco paisajes tiene el ojo
Estos paisajes cantarán solos el día del gran triunfo
Cantarán con la alegría de sus árboles tremolantes
Porque cayeron las cabezas de todos los espectros
Porque ya desangraron todos los fantasmas
Y se cerraron los ojos que tenían látigos
Y las bocas antropófagas de dientes arrogantes
Ahora se puede cantar
Millones de hombres pueden cantar
Un canto inmenso como una montaña que trepa por el cielo
Se soltaron las canciones amarradas
Y el viento les dió la dirección de su esperanza

Trescientas sesenta y cinco canciones suben al espacio
Canciones con los ojos azules

They walk with their hands in their pockets
With arrogance in the dent of their hats
And a lash in each eye
They walk along in their shoes luminous as coffins
They walk along like coffins in their coffins

Those specters live on the blood of millions of men
And because they live in life life is hateful
And men prefer death
Death with its movement that never gets rusty

I I I

The sky has three hundred and sixty-five birds
These birds shall be banners the day of the great triumph
When men shall hear the hour of man singing
When no one lives from the strength born in the breasts of
    others
When no one is nourished on alien flesh
Nor breathes through alien lungs
Nor ties up his trousers with a slave's guts

The eye has three hundred and sixty-five landscapes
These landscapes shall sing solos the day of the great triumph
They shall sing with the joy of their waving trees
Because the heads of all the specters have fallen
Because all the fantoms are bloodless
And the eyes with lashes in them are closed
And the man-eating mouths with arrogant teeth
Now there can be singing
Millions of men can sing
A song as huge as a mountain that mounts through the sky
Songs in bondage have been loosed
The wind gave them the direction of its hope

Three hundred and sixty-five songs rise to the sky
Songs with blue eyes

Canciones con los ojos negros
Canciones con árboles gigantescos
Canciones con olas infatigables

Los dientes de los hombres ríen como los dientes de los niños
Cuando hablan en secreto a las niñas
El sol sale con traje nuevo a su trabajo diario
Los árboles suben hasta su propia punta sin descanso
Las olas chillan y se dan vueltas de carnero
Y los niños cantan
El sol cabizbajo
Sonando el badajo
Salió esta mañana
Muy tieso y muy majo
Con el cielo a cuestas
Y una nube al fajo

Murió el fantasma que se nutría de pulmones
Las canciones sueltan sus amarras por los mares libres
Murió el vampiro que sorbía los globos de la luz
Las flores lanzan campanadas sobre el mundo
Murieron las aves de rapiña en su leyenda negra
Las olas juegan como los niños
Murió el señor de las batallas y la señora de las llagas
Los árboles bailan tomados de la mano
El viento nuevo borró todas las fronteras
Las fronteras dijeron adiós y dieron el último suspiro
La tierra las enterró bajo la tierra

Así es agradable la vida
Y la vida aplaude a la vida
Las sonrisas aplauden al viento
Las canciones aplauden a los pájaros
Los pájaros aplauden a la luz
La luz aplaude a los árboles
Los árboles aplauden al cielo

Songs with black eyes
Songs with gigantic trees
Songs with untiring waves

Men's teeth laugh like boys' teeth
When they secretly talk with girls
The sun goes to its daily toil with a new suit
The trees climb to their own tops without resting
The waves shriek and turn cartwheels
And the children sing
The melancholy sun
Ringing his bell
Came forth this morning
Very erect and well groomed
With the sky on his back
And a cloud in his girdle

The fantom that lived on lungs is dead
Songs loosen their bonds in the liberated seas
The vampire that sucked the spheres of light is dead
The flowers fling bell strokes over the world
The birds of prey are dead in their black legend
The waves play like children
The lord of battles is dead and the lady of ulcers
The trees dance holding hands
The new wind has erased all frontiers
The frontiers have said good-by and drawn their last breath
The earth buries them under the earth

So life is pleasant
And life applauds life
Smiles applaud the wind
Song applauds the birds
The birds applaud the light
The light applauds the trees
The trees applaud the sky

El cielo aplaude al sol
El sol aplaude a las olas

Y toda la vida es un teatro de aplausos
Así es agradable la vida y puede bailar como las flores
Que sueltan sus colores y sus perfumes de alegría

Ver y palpar

The sky applauds the sun
The sun applauds the waves

And all of life is a theater full of applause
So life is pleasant and can dance like the flowers
That unloose their colors and their perfumes of joy

EUGENIO FLORIT

b. 1903, Madrid, Spain

E U G E N I O   F L O R I T

b. 1903, Madrid, Spain

F LORIT'S early years were spent in Spain, in Madrid and Barcelona. His mother, however, is Cuban and in 1918 the family moved to Cuba where the poet studied law. After he became a Cuban citizen in 1922 he entered the service of the State Department. At this time he was associated with the group of the *Revista de avance*. In 1936 he met the Spanish poet, Juan Ramón Jiménez, who had a profound effect upon his work. Since 1940 Florit has been employed in the Cuban consulate in New York City and since 1941 he has also been teaching in the Spanish department of Columbia University. Florit's poetry is notable for its purity of style and delicacy of texture. He first perfected himself in the traditional forms; the *décimas* (ten-line stanzas) of *Trópico* are rigorously chiseled and his sonnets show him in perfect control of conventional poetic technique. His later poems are freer in form and their character varies from classical simplicity to an almost baroque complication of detail. A somewhat mystical quality relates Florit's work to contemporary Spanish poetry, while a dreamlike ecstatic mood indicates his debt to the English romantics, especially Keats and Shelley. It is to be expected that a Cuban poet should be impressed by the sea and the sea contributes a rich variety of symbols to much of his verse. He is a neo-symbolist in the sense that he is preoccupied with subtle spiritual values, that he is filled with a burning desire to penetrate to the essence of experience. There are few Spanish American poets who can be compared with Florit for graceful artistry.

The poem "Elegía para tu ausencia" was written after the

death of the poet's father. It illustrates how Florit transforms
actual experience into a pattern of symbols, intensifying it
on a high imaginative plane. "La señal" and "Atlántico" mark
the two poles of his work, the former a simple direct state-
ment, the latter an impressionist elaboration of detail.
"Tarde presente" reveals his most Spanish quality of mystical
exaltation.

32 poemas breves. Havana, 1927.
Trópico. Havana, 1930.
Doble acento. Havana, 1937.
Reino. Havana, 1938.
Cuatro poemas. Havana, 1940.

NOCTURNO

Corazón de mis noches:
desnudo de palabras,
hecho sobre las ascuas
de recuerdos y goces.

Hundido en el desierto
de arenas indecisas,
con aguas amarillas
en oasis de sueños.

Saber que voy desnudo
bajo miles de estrellas
y sentir cómo tiembla
el dolor en el mundo.

Navego por las horas
que más sufren el frío
de un paisaje vivido
más allá de estas cosas.

Huir en la corriente
por la mitad del alma,
que se acerca en la blanca
inquietud de esta muerte.

Qué ríos me atraviesan
de frías aguas tímidas,
y cómo va la risa
cayéndose en estrellas.

Doble acento (1937)

NOCTURNE

Heart of my nights:
Naked of words,
Fashioned over the coals
Of pleasures and memories.

Immersed in the desert
Of irresolute sands
With yellow waters
In oasis of dreams.

To know that I go naked
Under thousands of stars
And to feel how sorrow
Trembles in the world.

I sail through the hours
That suffer most from the cold
Of a landscape lived
Beyond these things.

To escape in the current
Through the center of the soul
That approaches in the white
Inquietude of this death.

What rivers of cold,
Timid waters traverse me,
What laughter there is
Falling in stars!

ELEGIA PARA TU AUSENCIA

"Peace, peace, he is not dead, he doth not sleep.
He hath awakened from the dream of life."
                                                    Shelley.

Te fuiste aquel minuto para toda la muerte
a navegar en hondos océanos de silencio
con un largo camino de pupilas dormidas
y un bando de palomas prendido a tus ensueños.

Ya estarás por ausentes claridades de luna,
más tuyo que en las flechas de tu reloj de oro,
donde contabas tanto minuto sin orillas
para la sed de alas que quemaba tus hombros.

Y habrás saltado mares que la inquietud miraba,
abismos en la tímida soledad de tu ausencia;
y en la noche habrás sido tenue brisa caliente
junto a aquel pedacito de tu amorosa tierra.

Largo abrazo de alientos sobre las amapolas
y una risa, y un canto sin palabras ni música;
y un aquí estoy gozoso de pasados insomnios,
y un para siempre cálido en la fría llanura.

Como partiste en brazos del silencio apretado,
resonará más viva la luz de tus palabras;
y en cada estrofa de aire se enredará un acento,
y en cada mariposa te nacerán más alas.

Gozo de estar ya vivo para el eterno día,
de saberte en el agua, y en el sol, y en la hierba.
Harás entre las nubes Nacimientos de plata
y encontrarás tu nido en un árbol de estrellas.

                                                    Doble acento

ELEGY FOR YOUR ABSENCE

In that moment you sailed for all of death
Into profound oceans of silence
With long hours of sleeping pupils,
And a flock of doves caught in your dreams.

Now you are already in distant moonlight,
More yourself than in the arrows of your golden clock
Where you reckoned such a shoreless moment
For the thirst of wings that was burning on your shoulders.

You shall have vaulted seas stared at by inquietude,
Abysses in the timid solitude of your absence;
And in the night you shall have been delicate warm breeze
Close to that crumb of your amorous earth.

Long embrace of breath over the poppies
And a laugh and a song without words or music;
With a "Here I am," glad of past wakefulness,
And a "forever" warm in the cool plain.

As you leave pressed in the arms of silence
The light of your words shall echo more clearly
And in each stanza of air an accent shall be entangled
And in each butterfly more wings shall be born to you.

Gladness of being alive for that eternal day,
Knowing yourself in the water, in the sun, and in the grass.
Among the clouds you shall make nativities of silver
And you shall discover your nest in a tree of stars.

LA NEREIDA MUERTA

A Emilio Ballagas

Comba del Mediodía
sobre mar de silencio.
¿Cómo fué la agonía,
Nereida, de tu muerte?

Mitad de sol y luna,
de estrellas y de nubes,
mitad de algas y arenas,
de coral encendido
y de piedras salobres.
Siempre mitad de brisa
por la tierra y el agua.

(¿Cómo estás, sola y una
en la muerte, Nereida?)

Torso inútil, ahora
ribera de cabellos;
un minuto de soles
con el aéreo juego.
Homenaje de conchas
a tu callada muerte
se junta por el rastro
de un caracol vacío.

Soledad de la espina
tan lejos de su veste,
devorada—tan tierna—
en bocas de otros peces.

Así mirada, apenas
se recuerdan las manos,
que al sol, peines de nácar,

THE DEAD NEREID

To Emilio Ballagas

Bulge of midday
Over sea of silence.
What was the agony
Of your death, Nereid?

Half sun, half moonlight,
Half stars, half clouds,
Half sand and seaweeds,
Half reddened corals,
Half salt-covered stones,
Always half breeze
On land and on water.

(How single and alone you are
In death, Nereid!)

Vain torso, now
Shore of tresses;
Moment of suns
In the airy sport.
Homage of shells
For your silent death
Collects in the trail
Of an empty sea snail.

Solitude of the spine
So far from its vesture—
So tender—devoured—
By other fish mouths.

Seen thus, your hands
Are scarcely remembered,
Pearly combs, polishing,

alisaban ensueños;
quietas ya, desvalidas,
huérfanas del acento
nacido en sus entrañas
para lumbre del eco.

Sal en la boca seca
—único don marino
con reflejo de nubes
en cada gota de agua
que en el viento resbala.

Risa de las espumas,
ya tímido su acento,
queda en la cola, ausente
rumor de rezo amargo,
para llegar sin alas
a los muertos oídos.

(Que destino tenías
de morir desmarada.
Qué ausencia, ya sin término,
por nuevos océanos.)

Rumor ensangrentado
en las pupilas duerme.
Fuego de intactos soles
a escalas de la brisa
por agujas de asombro.
La risa, desde el sueño,
eco de antiguas ondas,
vive en callado pecho.

Soledad bajo el canto
de estrellas apagadas.
Ya del minuto cálido
se escapan lejanías.

Dreams in sunlight;
Quiet, now, helpless,
Orphaned of the accent
Born within them
For the echo's glitter.

Salt in the dry mouth—
Single sea gift
With cloud reflections
In each drop of water
That slides in the wind.

Laughter of sea foam,
Timidly its accent
Still lingers in the tail,
Empty murmur of bitter prayer
That mounts without wings
To lifeless ears.

(What a destiny was yours
To die stranded.
What absence still endless
In new oceans!)

Bloodstained murmur
Sleeps in the pupils.
Fire of intact suns
On ladders of breeze,
Up needles of amazement.
Laughter from the dream,
Echo of antique rollers,
Lives in the silent breast.

Solitude under the song
Of extinguished stars.
Now from the warm moment
Distances are flying.

Todo el Dios humillado
por designio de luces
llora espumas ardientes
y suspiros de brisa.

Padre Dios alza brazos
sobre mudas arenas
por tocar, deslizándose,
un recuerdo sin alma.

Qué muda ya, despojo
derribado, qué frías
escamas, qué serena
la carne retadora
de la noche y el viento.

Y qué solas, al tiempo
de recordarte viva,
las ondas sin jinete
bajo el cielo se alargan.

Doble acento

ATLANTICO

¿Cuál de tus olas es ésta que viene tan niña
por el salto en la cuerda del Golfo,
y la resonancia del viaje dormido sin norte
para cuna de peces con fuego solar en la escama?

Tuvo una historia por sueños de luna,
cuando subían las flores marinas a prenderse en su pecho.
Tanto germen de madera, y botones de nácar, y cráneos
florecidos en árboles verdes con frutas de un oro olvidado.

¿Qué he de hacer, si la veo jugar con un niño,
sino olvidarme de que cubría infiernos con su sonrisa inter-
minable?

All of the God humbled
In a pattern of lights
Weeps burning sea foam
And sighs of breeze.

God the Father heaves up
Arms over mute sands,
Gliding to touch
A soulless memory.

Abandoned remains,
How mute now, how coldly
Scaly, how serene
The flesh, challenger
Of the wind and the nighttime.

And how lonely, whenever
They remember you living,
The riderless rollers
Stretch under the sky.

ATLANTIC

Which of your waves is it that comes so childlike,
Skipping the rope of the Gulf,
And the resonance of the poleless, sleeping voyage
As a cradle for fish with sun fire in their scales?

It had a history through dreams of moonlight
When seaflowers rose to adorn its breast.
What a source of wood and pearl buttons and skulls
Flowering in green trees with fruits of forgotten gold.

What should I do if I see it play with a child
Except to forget that hells are concealed in its endless smile?

Tendrá su castigo en cristal encerrada con inmóvil arena,
perdida la luz, y el ensueño, y la luna, y la muerte.

Retrato de nube y alambre de fuego en la arista
¿ésa es, sin aliento, cegada por múltiples uñas?
Y ahora recuerdo: voy a saber si aquel continente perdido
. . . Pero la caricia y la voz son aún más hermosas.
Esta ola que no sabe nada guarda tanto recuerdo.
Voy a saber si aquel continente . . . ¿Qué caballo asfixiado
en el vientre del buque relinchó al mirar su agonía?
Ha de tener un remordimiento por cada espanto del ojo
puesto a rodar en el fondo impreciso del agua.

Voy a saber si aquel . . . Entre los cocos y Platón,
y el olivo, y el trébol, y la foca, y el salvaje desnudo,
tienen suspendida esa sábana para mantear una estrella.
Si la hunden un poco, ¿no puede clavarse en la punta
de un mástil que sueña hace tres siglos con sus San Telmos?

Voy a saber . . . Tengo prisa por soltar esta ola.
Allá va. Cógela tú, hombre de las Islas Azores.
¿No es cierto que iba saltando en la escama de un pez
                                                    volador?

Doble acento

It shall have its punishment enclosed with motionless sand
     in crystal,
The light lost and the dream and the moon and death.

Portrait of cloud and copper with fire in its bevel,
Is it blinded by multiple claws, deprived of breath?
And now I remember: I shall know if that lost continent . . .
But the tenderness and the voice are even more beautiful.
This wave that knows nothing keeps so much memory.
I shall know if that continent . . . what horse stifled
In the hold of the ship neighed feeling its agony?
The wave must be filled with remorse for each fear the eye
     feels,
Set roving in the cloudy depths of the sea.

I shall know if that . . . Between the coconuts and Plato,
And the olive and the clover and the seal and the naked
     savage,
They hold this blanket suspended to toss up a star.
If they sink it a little, can it not be nailed to the tip
Of a mast that sleeps three centuries with its Saint Elmo's
     fire?

I shall know . . . I hasten to leap this wave.
There it goes. Catch it, man of the Azores.
Did it not go leaping, surely, in the scale of a flying fish?

AQUARIUM

Cerca del mar—tan lejos—
en cal y muerta arena,
albatros en prisión, adormecido.
Qué anhelo de volar sobre la espuma
de un libre mar, con horas libres.

Lejos,—tan cerca—el natural camino,
pueblo de quillas y alas tensas.
Y la risa, en el sol, bajo la luna,
a la seca prisión llega, cantando.

Aquí, por toda suerte,
por pequeña ventura,
por ilusión de ruta,
en la entraña esta vida
de agua infeliz, pez solo,
abandonada concha, vacía de su sueño.

Toda la luz, perdida;
la caricia del mar, para otras naves
libres, al beso claro de los vientos.

Y, en la alta noche, tímido, un suspiro
al mar abierto, a la brillante espuma,
por camino de cal y muerta arena.

Reino (1938)

A Q U A R I U M

Close to the sea—so far—
In lime and dead sand,
Imprisoned albatross, in a doze.
What yearning to fly over the foam
Of a free sea in hours of liberty!

Far—so near—their natural road,
People of keels and taut wings.
And the laughter, in sunlight, under the moon
Comes singing into the dry prison.

Here, for better or for worse,
Through fortune's avarice,
As an illusion of the highway,
In its core, this life
Of unhappy water, lonely fish,
Abandoned shell, empty of its dream.

All the light lost;
The tenderness of the sea, free to other ships,
In the clear kiss of the winds.

And, in the deep night, timidly, a sigh
For the open sea, for the brilliant foam,
By way of lime and dead sand.

LA SEÑAL

Sobre la risa, mar,
sobre las alegrías de colores,
sobre la estrofa azul y verde
y sobre aquella cinta blanca;
sobre el fondo amarillo con sol de mediodía,
sobre la noche y sobre el gris cerrado bajo el cielo,
siempre la gaviota,
alta, y baja después, de nube al agua,
de ala tendida y de caricia breve:
espíritu, señal graciosa del espíritu
sobre la risa abierta de la onda.

Reino

TARDE PRESENTE

Entre el ocaso y yo, toda la vida.
Como si detenido
el tiempo se cayera
a florecer en una gota de agua.
Como si Dios en su alto pensamiento
secara el llanto de sus hijos;
y Ella, la sin color, durmiera al borde florecido
de sus innumerables tumbas.
Como si ayer llegara con su recuerdo escrito
y mañana estuviera ya en su cárcel de letras;
como si hoy fuera una enorme rosa
de millones de pétalos unidos
en una sola esquina del mundo revelado.
O aún mejor: como si todo beso
de amante hubiera roto su semilla
y se alzaran al viento del crepúsculo
sus alas libres.
          Como el vuelo
apretado de ejércitos de ángeles

THE SIGNAL

Above the laughter, O sea,
Above the delights of colors,
Above the blue and green stanza
And above the white ribbon;
Above the yellow depth with the midday sun,
Above the night and above the gray locked under the sky,
Always the seagull
Rises and falls again from cloud to water
On outstretched wing and fleeting tenderness:
Spirit, gracious signal of the spirit,
Above the open laughter of the wave.

THE PRESENT EVENING

Between me and the sunset, the whole of life.
As if time, arrested,
Were falling
To blossom in a drop of water.
As if God in his lofty meditation
Were drying the tears of his sons;
And She, the colorless one, were sleeping on the flowering
        border
Of her innumerable tombs.
As if yesterday were to come with its written memory
And tomorrow were already in its prison of letters;
As if today were an enormous rose
Of millions of petals, united
In a single corner of the revealed world.
Or better still; as if all lovers' kisses
Had burst from their seedbed
And were raising in the twilight wind
Their liberated wings.
                        Like the compact flight
Of armies of angels

en su más alto círculo.
Como ascensión de un pensamiento libre
hasta el principio
donde nació la luz y se formaron
entraña de dolor, gérmen de grito
y lágrima primera bajo el cielo.
Como si todo junto de repente
se pusiera entre el hombre y su destino.
Como si ante el ocaso rojo abriera
un girasol sus rayos amarillos.
Como si aquella mano
de ayer regara azules lirios
y fuera el mar bajo la mano
un palomar de pétalos heridos.
Y como si los barcos emergieran
de su muerte de hierros, de su sueño
de peces, de su olvido,
para tender sus velas inmortales
a los vientos y al sol.
        Como si fríos
los huesos de la tierra,
por fuego inmaterial enrojecidos
hasta el blanco del alma
volvieran a pesar, a estremecerse,
a reír y a llorar, en risa y llanto
de verdad, en latidos
de pecho verdadero, en ojos limpios,
en bocas sin pecado, en tibia
caricia de sus carnes.
        Así dicho
frente al ocaso, desde tierra al mar,
con la ternura junto a mí.
        Se alegra
el corazón de manso gris vestido.

        Cuatro poemas (1940)

In their highest sphere.
Like the ascension of a thought at liberty
Toward the source
Where light is born and the core of sorrow,
The germ of a cry and a first tear
Have taken form under the sky.
As if all of this together suddenly
Intervened between man and his destiny.
As if a sunflower were opening its yellow petals
In front of the red west.
As if the hand of yesterday
Were sprinkling blue lilies
And the sea beneath the hand
Were a dovecote of wounded petals.
And as if the ships were emerging
From their dead iron, from their dream of fishes,
From their oblivion
To stretch their immortal sails
In the winds and the sun.
                    As if the cold
Bones of the earth,
Reddened by immaterial fire,
Were returning to the white heat of the soul
To ponder, to tremble,
To laugh, and to weep, with laughter and tears
Of truth, in the beating
Of an actual breast, in clean eyes,
In sinless mouths, in the warm
Caress of its flesh.
                    These words,
Facing the west, from sea to sky,
With tenderness close to me.
                    The heart,
Dressed in gray humility, rejoices.

LA MUERTE EN EL SOL

La silenciosa luz traspasa los cristales.
Y en el aire templado de este otoño
afuera hay, con el sol y las palomas,
música militar y marchas serias.
Y adentro, en el silencio claro,
tan lejos ¡ay! estamos, tan perdidos,
que apenas por el toque del reloj
recordamos que hay tiempo.
Y que es tiempo de horror, tiempo de muerte
allá donde la luz será como ésta,
y donde, no como éstas, las palomas
mueren en el veneno de los aires.
Y los hombres terminan.
Y todo se hunde en el terror.
Ese terror de recibir la muerte
en un día de sol
como este sol de aquí,
—con la luz silenciosa de este otoño.

Poemas no coleccionados

D E A T H   I N   T H E   S U N

The silent light penetrates the panes.
And in the mild air of this autumn,
Outside with the sun and the pigeons,
There is military music and solemn marching.
And within, in the clear silence,
We are so distant, ah, so lost,
That scarcely by the ticking of the clock
Do we remember that time exists.
And that it is a time of horror, a time of death
Over there where the light will be like this
And where, not like these, the pigeons die
In the poison of the winds.
And men meet their end.
And all is submerged in terror.
That terror of receiving death
On a sunny day
As sunny as this one,
With the silent light of this autumn.

JORGE LUIS BORGES

b. 1900, Buenos Aires, Argentina

JORGE LUIS BORGES

b. 1900, Buenos Aires, Argentina

THE career of Borges is divided into two parts. He studied in the College of Geneva, Switzerland, during the first World War and at the end of the war went to Spain. While he lived in Madrid he was associated with Rafael Cansinos Assens and Guillermo de Torre at the time when the ultraist movement was at its height. He wrote ultraist poems and became a theorist of the movement. None of these early poems were published in book form. When he returned to Buenos Aires in 1921 his work changed completely. Repatriation caused him to rediscover his own country. Breaking with ultraism, he became a nationalist with the avowed intention of interpreting his people and their traditions. He helped found the reviews *Prisma* and *Proa* and in the latter published many essays on literary subjects during the early 'twenties. His influence as a poet, critic, and editor had much to do with the contemporary renaissance in Argentinian poetry. It is probably because of his influence that so many of the younger Argentinian poets are nationalists. He stimulated young writers by his technical criticism and translated distinguished foreign writers such as Kafka, Gide, Virginia Woolf, Joyce, and Faulkner. In recent years he has abandoned poetry for prose. Borges is the poet of Buenos Aires. He leans toward the philosophic, interpreting the city with both love and revulsion. Some critics have considered him to be influenced by the seventeenth-century Spanish poet, Quevedo. He is a realist in the sense that he makes use of his immediate environment in poetry, but he is not a naturalist. There is considerable romantic symbolism woven into the texture of his verses. His use of unusual metaphors recalls his early apprenticeship to ultraism. In form his poetry is not extremely radical. Borges represents the Europeanized culture of the greatest metropolis in South America.

An especially interesting example of Borges' nationalism is the poem dealing with General Quiroga. This refers to an episode in Argentinian history. Juan Manuel Rosas was a dictator controlling La Plata provinces in the early nineteenth century, and Facundo Quiroga (b. 1790) was a rising *caudillo,* subordinate to Rosas, who had gained control of several provinces. Both were noted for their cruelty. Fearing Quiroga as a rival, Rosas had him assassinated in 1835 at Barranca Yaco. Quiroga was a gaucho leader, and Argentina has a whole literature (folk songs, novels, and plays) dealing with gaucho life which parallels our wild west songs and stories. The Argentinian romantic Sarmiento also wrote a bitter biography of Quiroga in 1845 immortalizing him as a symbol of brutal despotism. This has become one of the most famous books in all South American literature. Borges is therefore using very familiar traditional material. His poem about Quiroga has something of the popular ballad quality.

Fervor de Buenos Aires. Buenos Aires, 1923.
Luna de enfrente. Buenos Aires, 1925.
Inquisiciones (essays). Buenos Aires, 1925.
El tamaño de mi esperanza (prose). Buenos Aires, 1926.
El idioma de los argentinos (essays). Buenos Aires, 1928.
Cuaderno San Martín. Buenos Aires, 1929.
Evaristo Carriego (prose). Buenos Aires, 1930.
Discusión (prose). Buenos Aires, 1932.
La Kenningar (prose). Buenos Aires, 1933.
Historia de la infamia (prose). Buenos Aires, 1935.

UN PATIO

Con la tarde
se cansaron los dos o tres colores del patio.
La gran franqueza de la luna llena
ya no entusiasma su habitual firmamento.
Hoy que está crespo el cielo
dirá la agorería que ha muerto un angelito.
Patio, cielo encauzado.
El patio es la ventana
por donde Dios mira las almas.
El patio es el declive
por el cual se derrama el cielo en la casa.
Serena
la eternidad espera en la encrucijada de estrellas.
Lindo es vivir en la amistad oscura
de un zaguán, de un alero y de un aljibe.

Fervor de Buenos Aires (1923)

CARNICERIA

Más vil que un lupanar
la carnicería rubrica como una afrenta la calle.
Sobre el dintel
la esculpidura de una cabeza de vaca
de mirar ciego y cornamenta grandiosa
preside el aquelarre
de carne charra y mármoles finales
con la lejana majestad de un ídolo
o con la fijeza impasible
de la palabra escrita junto a la palabra que se habla.

Fervor de Buenos Aires

A PATIO

At evening
The two or three colors of the patio grow tired.
The great frankness of the full moon
No longer fills its habitual firmament with enthusiasm.
Since the sky is rippled today
The augurs will say that a little angel has died.
Patio, channel of sky.
The patio is the window
Through which God looks at souls.
The patio is the slope
Down which the sky pours into the house.
Serene,
Eternity waits in the intersection of the stars.
It is pleasant to live in the obscure friendship
Of a vestibule, of the eaves, and of a cistern.

BUTCHER SHOP

Meaner than a brothel
The butcher shop defaces the street like an insult.
Above the lintel
The sculptured head of a steer,
With blind stare and grandiose horns
Presides over the witches' Sabbath
Of coarse flesh and final marbles
With the distant majesty of an idol
Or with the impassible fixity
Of the written word next to the spoken.

BENARES

Falsa y tupida
como un jardín calcado en un espejo,
la urbe imaginada
que mis pisadas no conocen
entreteje hurañas distancias
y repite sus casas
como una boca que repite plegarias.
El sol salvaje
semejante a la decisiva zarpa de un tigre
desgarra la oscuridad maciza
de templos, muladares, cárceles, patios
y ha de estrujar los muros
de colores borrachos
y colgar de los hombros escurridizos
mochilas de calor.
Jadeante
la ciudad que oprimió un follaje de estrellas
desborda el horizonte
cual una piedra agujereando un estanque
y en la mañana llena
de pasos y de sueño
la luz va abriendo como ramas las calles.
La selva
donde grita el hedor de la alimaña
naufraga lejos encallada
contra los arrecifes
de un aurora en jirones,
mientras juntamente amanece
en las persianas todas que miran al oriente
y la voz de un almuédano
que ya rezó el disperso rosario de los astros
apesadumbra desde su alta torre
la leve madrugada.
(Y pensar
que mientras brujuleo las imágenes

BENARES

Counterfeit and choked up,
Like a garden traced in a mirror,
The imagined city,
Unknown to my footsteps,
Weaves shy distances
And repeats its houses
Like a mouth repeating prayers.
The savage sun like the sure claw of a tiger
Tears the massive obscurity
Of temples, dungheaps, prisons, patios
And must crush the walls
With drunken colors
And hang knapsacks of heat
On slippery shoulders.
Panting,
The city, weighed down by a foliage of stars,
Overflows the horizon
Like a stone piercing a pond
And in the morning
Full of footsteps and sleep
The light goes opening the streets like branches.
The forest,
Where the stench of beasts cries out,
Is wrecked far off, run aground
On the reefs
Of a tattered dawn,
While at the same time day breaks
In all the shutters facing the east
And the voice of a muezzin,
Which has already mumbled the scattered rosary of the stars,
Mourns the fragile sunrise
From its high tower.
(And to think
That while I reveal the images,

la ciudad que canto, persiste
sobre la espalda del mundo
con sus visiones ineludibles y fijas
repleta como un sueño
con agresiones de injuriosa miseria
con arrabales y cuarteles
y hombres de labios podridos
que sienten frío en los dientes.)

Fervor de Buenos Aires

LA RECOLETA

Convencidos de caducidad
vueltos un poco irreales por el morir altivado en tanto
sepulcro
irrealizados por tanta grave certidumbre de muerte,
nos demoramos en las veredas
que apartan los panteones enfilados
cuya vanilocuencia
hecha de mármol, de rectitud y sombra interior
equivale a sentencias axiomáticas y severas
de Manrique o de Fray Luis de Granada.
Hermosa es la serena decisión de las tumbas,
su arquitectura sin rodeos
y las plazuelas donde hay frescura de patio
y el aislamiento y la individuación eternales;
cada cual fué contemplador de su muerte
única y personal como un recuerdo.
Nos place la quietud,
equivocamos tal paz de vida con el morir
y mientras creemos anhelar el no-ser
lanzamos jaculatorias a la vida apacible.
Vehemente en las batallas y remansado en las losas
sólo el vivir existe.
Son aledaños suyos tiempo y espacio,
son arrabales de alma

The city that I sing endures
On the shoulder of the world
With its fixed and inevitable visions,
Filled like a dream
With assaults of disdainful poverty,
With slums and wards
And men with rotten lips
That feel the cold in their teeth.)

T H E   R E C O L E T A *

Convinced of frailty, death
Turned a little unreal by dying exalted in so much sepulcher,
Unfulfilled by so much serious certainty of death,
We linger in the paths
That separate the files of pantheons
Whose eloquence,
Made of marble, of rectitude and of shadows inside,
Equals the axiomatic and severe sentences
Of Manrique or Fray Luis de Granada.†
The serene decision of the tombs is beautiful,
Their uncompromising architecture
And the little squares with the coolness of a patio
And the isolation and eternal individuation;
Each contemplated his own death,
Unique and personal like a memory.
The quietude pleases us,
We confuse such peace in life with dying
And while we believe we desire not to be
We are praying for a peaceful life.
Eager in battle, stagnant under the stones,
Only living exists.
Its boundaries are time and space,
They are slums of the soul,

* La Recoleta is the name of a cemetery in Buenos Aires.
† Jorge Manrique (1440–70) was a Spanish lyric poet famous for his
Coplas por la muerte de su padre. Fray Luis de Granada (1504–88) was a
Spanish Dominican well known for his devotional prose.

son las herramientas y son las manos del alma
y en desbaratándose esta,
juntamente caducan el espacio, el tiempo, el morir,
como al cesar la luz
se acalla el simulacro de los espejos
que ya la tarde fué entristeciendo.
Sombra sonora de los árboles,
viento rico en pájaros que sobre las ramas ondea,
alma mía que se desparrama por corazones y calles,
fuera milagro que alguna vez dejaran de ser,
milagro incomprensible, inaudito
aunque su presunta repetición abarque con grave horror la
    existencia.
Lo anterior: escuchado, leído, meditado
lo realicé en la Recoleta,
junto al proprio lugar donde han de enterrarme.

Fervor de Buenos Aires

S I N G L A D U R A

El mar es una espada innumerable y una plenitud de pobreza.
La llamarada es traducible en ira, todo manantial en fuga-
    cidad, cualquier cisterna en clara aceptación.
El mar es solitario como un ciego.
El mar es un huraño lenguaje que yo no alcanzo a descifrar.
En su hondura, el alba es una humilde tapia encalada.
De su confín surge el claror igual que una humareda o un
    vuelo de calandrias.
Impenetrable como de piedra labrada persiste el mar ante los
    ágiles días.
Cada tarde es un puerto.
Nuestra mirada flagelada de mar camina por su cielo:
Ultima playa blanda, celeste arcilla de las tardes urbanas.
¡Qué dulce intimidad la del ocaso en el huraño mar!
Claras como un feria brillan las nubes y hay mansedumbres
    de suburbio en su gracia.

They are the tools and hands of the soul
And when this crumbles
Space and time and dying decay together,
As when the light ceases the simulacrum
In the mirrors grows dim,
Already saddened by the evening.
Sonorous shadow of trees,
Wind rich in birds that ripples over the branches,
My soul which is scattered among hearts and streets,
It would be a miracle that some time they should cease to be,
Unheard incomprehensible miracle,
Even though its presumed repetition comprises existence
    with grave horror.
What went before: heard, read, meditated,
I have realized in the Recoleta,
Next to the very spot where they are going to bury me.

A DAY'S RUN

The sea is an innumerable sword, an abundance of poverty.
The blaze can be translated into anger, all flux into fugacity,
    any pool into pure acceptance.
The sea is solitary as a blind man.
The sea is a shy language which I do not succeed in de-
    ciphering.
In its depth the dawn is a meek, whitewashed wall.
From its boundary arises the glare like a puff of smoke or a
    flight of skylarks.
Impenetrable as if cut from stone the sea goes on existing
    before the agile days.
Each afternoon is a harbor.
Our glance, flagellated by sea, travels through its sky:
Last smooth beach, celestial clay of city evenings.
What sweet intimacy of the sunset in the shy sea!
The clouds shine bright as a holiday and there are the gentle-
    nesses of a suburb in its grace.

Cielo de limpio atardecer: mar pueril de conseja que cabe en
                     las plazitas y en los patios.
La luna nueva se ha enroscado a un mástil.
La misma luna que dejamos bajo un arco de piedra y cuya luz
                     agraciará los sauzales.
La tarde es una corazonada de orilla.
En la cubierta, quietamente, yo comparto la tarde con mi
                     hermana como un trozo de pan.

Luna de enfrente (1925)

EL GENERAL QUIROGA VA EN COCHE AL MUERE

El madrejón desnudo ya sin una sé de agua
Y la luna atorrando por el frío del alba
Y el campo muerto de hambre, pobre como una araña

El coche se hamacaba rezongando la altura:
Un galerón enfático, enorme, funerario.
Cuatro tapaos con pinta de muerte en la negrura
Tironeaban seis miedos y un valor desvelado.

Junto a los postillones gineteaba un moreno.
Ir en coche a la muerte ¡que cosa más oronda!
El General Quiroga quiso entrar al infierno
Llevando seis o siete degollados de escolta.

Esa cordobesada bochinchera y ladina
(Meditaba Quiroga) qué ha de poder con mi alma?
Aquí estoy afianzando y metido en la vida
Como la estaca pampa bien metida en la pampa.

Yo que he sobrevivido a millares de tardes
Y cuyo nombre pone retemblor en las lanzas
No he de soltar la vida por estos pedregales.
¿Muere acaso el pampero, se mueren las espadas?

Sky of clean evening: sea childlike as a fairy story that fits
in little squares and patios.
The new moon has twisted itself around a mast.
The same moon that we left under a stone arch and whose
light shall lend grace to the willowgroves.
The evening is a presentiment of shore.
On deck, quietly, I divide the evening with my sister like
a bit of bread.

GENERAL QUIROGA RIDES TO DEATH IN A CARRIAGE

The bare twisted shrubbery without a drop of water
And the moon choking in the coldness of the dawn
And the land dead of hunger, poor as a spider,

The carriage was rocking, its top was grumbling
An energetic jig, huge and funereal.
Four masked riders, the color of death in their blackness
Were pulling six fears and one sleepless valor.

Close to the postillions a dark man was riding.
Riding to death in a carriage, what could be more pompous!
General Quiroga wished to make his entrance into hell
Bringing six or seven headless men to escort him.

That sly and ruffianly Cordovan gang
(Quiroga was reflecting) what can they do to me?
Here I am fastened, staked through the midst of life
Just like a picket driven deep into the pampa.

I who have survived thousands of evenings
And whose very name throws a shiver into the lances
Shan't loose my hold on life among these stony plains.
Does the south wind ever die, are not swords immortal?

Pero en llegando al sitio nombrao Barranca Yaco
Sables a filo y punta menudiaron sobre él:
Muerte de mala muerte se lo llevó al riojano
Y una de puñaladas lo mentó a Juan Manuel.

Luego (ya bien repuesto) penetró como un taita
En el infierno negro que Dios le hubo marcado
Y a sus órdenes iban, rotas y desangradas,
Las ánimas en pena de fletes y cristianos.

Luna de enfrente

EL PASEO DE JULIO

Juro que no por deliberación he vuelto a la calle
de alta recova repetida como un espejo,
de parrillas con la trenza de carne de los Corrales,
de prostitución encubierta por lo más distinto: la música.

Puerto mutilado sin mar, encajonada racha salobre,
resaca que te adheriste a la tierra: Paseo de Julio,
aunque recuerdos míos, antiguos hasta la ternura, te saben
nunca te sentí patria.

Sólo poseo de ti una deslumbrada ignorancia
una insegura propiedad como la de los pájaros en mi aire,
pero mi verso es de interrogación y de prueba
y para obedecer lo entrevisto.

Barrio con lucidez de pesadilla al pie de los otros,
tus espejos curvos denuncian el lado de la fealdad de las
    caras,
tu noche calentada en lupanares pende de la ciudad.

Eres la perdición fraguándose un mundo
con los reflejos y las deformaciones de éste;
sufres de caos, adoleces de irrealidad,

But arriving at a place called Barranca Yaco,
The point and edge of sabers struck him repeatedly
A very evil death came to the man from Rioja
A rain of dagger blows that spoke for Juan Manuel.

Then (already quite recovered) he went like a patriarch
Into the black hell that God had assigned him
And obedient to his orders there went with him the broken
And bloodless souls in torment of steeds and simple men.

JULY AVENUE

I swear I have not deliberately returned to the street
Of tall foodstands repeated like a mirror,
Of grills with the scrap of meat from the Corrales,*
Of prostitution concealed by what is most different: music.

Mutilated harbor without sea, boxed whiff of salt,
Surf sticking to the earth: July Avenue,
Though my memories, so old they grow tender, know you,
I never felt you as fatherland.

I only possess a dazzled ignorance of you,
An insecure property like that of the birds in my air,
But my verse is by way of question and trial
And in obedience to the encounter.

Ward at the foot of the city, sharp as a nightmare,
Your curved mirrors expose the ugly side of faces,
Your heated night hangs from the city in brothels.

You are perdition forging a world
With the reflections and deformities of this one;
You suffer from chaos, you are sick with unreality,

* The Corrales is a section of the city of Buenos Aires.

te empeñas en jugar con naipes raspados la vida;
tu alcohol mueve peleas,
tus griegas manosean libros envidiosos de magia.

¿Será porque el infierno es vacío
que es espuria tu misma fauna de monstruos
y la sirena prometida por ese cartel es muerta y de cera?

Tienes la inocencia terrible
de la resignación, del amanecer, del conocimiento,
la del espíritu no purificado, borrado.
por insistencias del destino
y que ya blanco de muchas luces, ya nadie,
sólo codicia lo presente, lo actual, como los hombres viejos.

Atrás de los paredones de mi suburbio, los duros carros
rezarán con varas en alto a su imposible dios de hierro y de
        polvo,
pero qué dios, qué ídolo, qué veneración la tuya, Paseo de
        Julio?

Tu vida pacta con la muerte;
toda felicidad, con sólo existir, te es adversa.
Paseo de Julio: Cielo para los que son del Infierno.

                                    Cuaderno San Martín (1929)

You persistently play for life with crooked cards,
Your drink provokes fist fights,
Your Greeks handle malignant books of magic.

Could it be, since hell is empty,
That your own fauna of monsters is counterfeit
And the siren this handbill promises is already dead and
    waxen?

You have the terrible innocence
Of resignation, of daybreak, of understanding,
That of a spirit unpurified, blotted
By the importunities of destiny
And which, already white with many lights, already a no-
    body,
Only covets the present, the actual, as old men do.

Behind the grillwork of my suburb, the rough wagons,
Shall pray with their shafts in the air to their impossible god
    of steel and dust,
But what god, what idol, what worship is yours, July Avenue?

Your life is a pact with death;
All happiness, merely existing, is contrary to you.
July Avenue: Heaven for those who come from hell.

FLUENCIA NATURAL DEL RECUERDO

Recuerdo mío del jardín de casa:
vida benigna de las plantas,
vida cortés de misteriosa
y lisonjeada por los hombres.

Palmera la más alta de aquel cielo
y conventillo de gorriones;
parra firmamental de uva negra,
los días del verano dormían a tu sombra.

Molino colorado:
remota rueda laboriosa en el viento,
honor de nuestra casa, pues a las otras
iba el río bajo la campanita del aguatero.

Sótano circular de la base
que hacías vertiginoso el jardín,
daba miedo entrever por una hendija
tu calabozo de agua sutil.

Jardín, frente a tu virtud retumbaron
los heroicos carreros criollos
y también el carnaval charro
con el ranchito y el candombe y el susto de agua.

El almacén, hermano del malevo,
dominaba la esquina;
pero tenías cañaverales para hacer lanzas
y gorriones para la oración.

El dormir de tus árboles y el mío
todavía en la oscuridad se amalgaman

NATURAL FLOW OF
MEMORY

My memory of the garden of our house:
Benignant life of the shrubbery,
Courteous life, by men made
Mysterious and pleasing.

Palm tree, the highest in that heaven
And tenement of sparrows,
Vine starred with black grapes;
The summer days were sleeping in your shadow.

Ruddy windmill:
Distant wheel industrious in the wind,
Pride of our house, since to the others
The river was borne beneath the little bell of the water seller.

Cellar, circular at the bottom,
Which made the garden dizzy,
And it frightened us to dimly see
Your dungeon of subtle water through a cranny.

Across from your virtue, garden,
The heroic creole carters rumbled
And also the coarse carnival
With the little hut, the *candombe** dancing, and the terror
    of water.

The warehouse, brother of the slum dweller,
Dominated the corner;
But you had cane fields to make lances
And sparrows for evening prayer.

My slumber and the slumber of your trees
Still blend together in the darkness

* Negro dance of African origin.

y la devastación de la urraca
dejó un antiguo miedo en mi sangre.

Tus contadas varas de fondo
se nos volvieron geografía:
un alto era "la montaña de tierra"
y una temeridad su declive.

Jardín, yo depondré mi oración
para seguir siempre acordándome
voluntad buena de dar sombra
fueron tus árboles.

Cuaderno San Martín

And the destruction of the magpie
Left an ancient fear in my blood.

Your few rods of length
Turned into our geography:
A hillock was "the mountain of earth"
And its slope foolhardiness.

Garden, I shall leave my evening prayer with you
To go on remembering always
The good will of your trees
That were our shade givers.

JORGE CARRERA ANDRADE

b. 1903, Quito, Ecuador

JORGE CARRERA ANDRADE

b. 1903, Quito, Ecuador

CARRERA ANDRADE began his literary career in his teens by editing a magazine, *La idea*. In 1928 he went abroad and studied in France, Germany, and Spain. He has been in the consular service of Ecuador in both Japan and China. During the 'thirties he lived in France and was editor of a publishing house in Paris, Cuadernos del Hombre Nuevo. At this time some of his poetry was translated into French by Edmond Vandercammen. Since 1940 he has been consul general for Ecuador in San Francisco. Of the Spanish classics, Góngora has had the most influence upon him, and in French literature he owes most to Francis Jammes. From the very beginning his style has been fully formed and all his books have mantained the same high level. Carrera Andrade never attempts the heroic: he is a miniaturist with exquisite taste and brilliant imagery. In *El tiempo manual* he uses Indian themes and is thus a precursor of the indigenist poetry which has now become a school. Certain of his later poems also show him moved by social protest; his sympathies are with the masses though the bulk of his poetry does not reflect a political point of view. Carrera Andrade is a poet of the senses. Like the American imagists he paints with words, rendering what he sees with the utmost precision. But he is not content with mere description; he intensifies his poetry with a flow of metaphors which add new dimensions to everything he records. His most recent poetry has grown more introspective; he seems to be seeking greater spiritual depth. An essayist as well as a poet, he writes, "Poetry is creation rather than construction. I do not believe it should be facility or craftsmanship . . . True poetry is

only that which has fallen from combat with the angel."
Carrera Andrade is generally considered to be the most
outstanding contemporary poet of Ecuador.

The poem "Tiempo ventoso" shows the influence of
Jammes. In its homely realism it is somewhat akin to post-
modernism. "Espejo del comedor" is typical of Carrera
Andrade's handling of a fragment of visual experience. It is
a three-dimensional still life which assumes profundity from
the intensity of the poet's perception. "Indiada" is a truly in-
digenist poem. "Islas sin nombre" is an example of his most
recent work which tends to grow increasingly symbolic.

Guirnalda del silencio. Quito, 1926.
Estanque inefable. Quito, 1926.
Boletines de mar y tierra. Barcelona, 1930.
Latitudes (essays). Quito, 1934; 2nd ed. Buenos Aires, 1940.
El tiempo manual. Madrid, 1935.
Biografía para uso de los pájaros. Paris, 1937.
Microgramas (essay and translations of Japanese hokku poems).
    Tokio, 1940.
País secreto. Pekin, 1940.
Registro del mundo (selected poems). Quito, 1940.
Canto al Puente de Oakland. San Francisco, 1941.

TIEMPO VENTOSO

Tengo ahora un maestro de alta literatura
que me ha enseñado a odiar todo lo escrito:
Es el viento del campo, un dulce viejecito
a quien los campesinos le llaman Don Ventura.

Don Ventura es maniático. Sale de madrugada
a buscar en los hierbas, húmedas, todavía,
la vara de virtud de la sabiduría.
Recorre el bosque hablando con su voz ya cascada.

Las frondas, de rodillas, le dan sus bendiciones.
Gime el cubo del pozo y el agua se estremece.
Luego, a la paz de un árbol, Don Ventura parece
un abate muy sabio que dicta sus lecciones.

Lee en el cielo cuándo va a llover, y procura
avisar en el pueblo llamando a cada puerta.
Los vecinos que viven con el oído alerta
se ponen a gritar: ¡Ya viene Don Ventura!

Guirnalda del silencio (1926)

BIOGRAFIA

La ventana nació de un deseo de cielo
y en la muralla negra se posó como un ángel.
Es amiga del hombre
y portera del aire.

Conversa con los charcos de la tierra,
con los espejos niños de las habitaciones
y con los tejados en huelga.

Desde su altura, las ventanas
orientan a las multitudes
con sus arengas diáfanas.

WINDY WEATHER

I now have a master of great literature
Who has taught me to hate all that is written:
It is the wind from the fields, a sweet old fellow
Whom the farmers call Milord Good Luck.

Milord Good Luck is crazy. He goes out in the morning
To seek the virtuous staff of knowledge
Among the still damp grasses.
He travels through the woods talking in a cracked voice.

On their knees the leaves give him their blessing.
The bucket in the well moans and the water trembles.
Then, under the peace of a tree, Milord Good Luck
Seems like a very learned abbé giving instructions.

He reads the sky when it is going to rain
And serves notice on the town, knocking at every door.
And the neighbors who have sharp ears
Begin to cry: Why here comes Milord Good Luck!

BIOGRAPHY

The window was born of a desire for sky
And stationed itself in the black wall like an angel.
It is friend to man
And a carrier of air.

It talks with pools of the earth
With the child mirrors of habitations
And with roofs in repose.

From their heights, the windows,
With their diaphanous harangues,
Are a landmark to the multitudes.

La ventana maestra
difunde sus luces en la noche.
Extrae la raíz cuadrada de un meteoro,
suma columnas de constelaciones.

La ventana es la borda del barco de la tierra,
la ciñe mansamente un oleaje de nubes.
El capitán Espíritu busca la isla de Dios
y los ojos se lavan en tormentas azules.

La ventana reparte entre todos los hombres
una cuarta de luz y un cubo de aire.
Ella es, arada de nubes,
la pequeña propiedad del cielo.

Boletines de mar y tierra (1930)

E S P E J O   D E   C O M E D O R

A Alfonso Reyes

Con escuadras y figuras
de cándida geometría,
el espejo de comedor
edifica.

Iza planos palpitantes
hasta su nivel azul.
Toma medida de las cosas
con sus compases de luz.

Baraja certidumbres.
Esgrime diámetros.
Enfila luces.

Hiere su regla de cristal
la botella de agua, desnuda,
y un chorro oblícuo de diamantes
mana hasta la mesa oscura.

The window, master of science,
Diffuses its light in the night.
It extracts the square root of a meteor,
Totals the columns of constellations.

The window is the gunwale of the ship of the earth,
A surf of clouds surrounds it.
Captain Spirit seeks the island of God
And his eyes are washed by blue tempests.

To all men the window distributes
A quart of light, a bucket of air.
Plowed by the clouds,
It is the small property of the sky.

DINING-ROOM MIRROR

To Alfonso Reyes

The dining-room mirror
Builds
With squares and figures
Of snowy geometry.

It hoists palpitant planes
Toward its blue level.
It takes the measure of objects
With its compasses of light.

It shuffles certainties.
It fences with diameters.
It lines up lights.

The naked water bottle
Breaks its crystal ruler
And a slanting stream of diamonds
Issues toward the dark table.

Los objetos
mueven en los hilos del aire
su telegrafía de reflejos.

Los colores estallan.
En las aristas felices
la luz bate las pestañas.

Piscina vertical
con diagonales de hielo.
Gemelos con la vida
los senos virginales del frutero.

Mundo animado
de resplandeciente conciencia.
Trigonometría de luces.
Visuales ideas.

La vida cortada en normas:
El salero es sapiencia;
las ostras, memoria.

La pera es escultura
en los moldes del aire;
el café, inteligencia
y el azucarero, un ángel.

Boletines de mar y tierra

Objects propel,
Along wires of air,
Their telegraphy of reflections.

The colors burst.
Light from the gay bevels
Strikes the eyelashes.

Vertical pools
With diagonals of ice.
Twins with the real,
The virginal breasts of the fruit bowl.

World, animated
With a glittering consciousness.
Trigonometry of light.
Visual ideas.

Life cut into patterns:
The saltcellar is wisdom;
The oysters, memory.

The pear is sculpture
In molds of air;
The coffee, intelligence,
And the sugar bowl, an angel.

CARTEL ELECTORAL DEL VERDE

Verde marino, almirante de los verdes.
Verde terrestre, camarada de los labradores,
innumerable anticipo de la felicidad de todos,
cielo infinito del ganado que pasta frescas eternidades.

Luz submarina del bosquecillo
donde plantas, insectos y pájaros viven consumiéndose
en el amor callado de un dios verde.
Olor verde de la carnosa cabuya
que en su marmita vegetal elabora
un profundo licor
hecho de lluvia y sombra.

Mesa tropical donde suda con su penacho verde
la cabeza tatuada de la piña.
Arbustos de jorobas verdes,
parientes pobres de las colinas.

Verde música de los insectos que cosen sin cesar
el paño grueso de la grama,
los zancudos que habitan en los violines
y el redoblar del opaco tamborcillo verde de la rana.

La verde cólera del cáctus
y la paciencia de los árboles que recogen en su red verde
una pesca milagrosa de pájaros.
Todo el verde aplacador del mundo
ahogándose en el mar, trepando las montañas hasta el cielo
y corriendo en el río—escuela de desnudez—
y en la vaca nostálgica del viento.

El tiempo manual (1935)

ELECTION HANDBILL OF GREEN

Seagreen, admiral of the greens,
Terrestrial green, comrade of the workers,
Numberless advance payments on everybody's happiness,
Infinite sky of livestock that pastures on cool eternities.

Submarine light of the shrubbery
Where plants, insects, and birds live languishing
In the silent love of a green god.
Green odor of fleshy hemp
Which manufactures a profound liquor
Out of rain and darkness
In its vegetable pot.

Tropical plateau where, with its green crest,
The tattooed head of the pineapple sweats,
Humpbacked green shrubs,
Poor relations of the hills.

Green music of insects that endlessly sew
The coarse cloth of the couch grass,
Waders that live in the violins
And the rolling of little, opaque, green frog drums.

The green anger of the cactus
And the patience of trees that gather
A miraculous catch of birds in their green net.
All the green appeasement of the world,
Drowning itself in the sea, climbing the mountains to the sky,
And running in the river—school for nudity—
And in the nostalgic cow which is the wind.

BOLETIN DEL MAL TIEMPO

El cielo del norte
levanta una bandera negra
en la barricada del horizonte.

No más oro de sol sobre los bancos.
¡Abajo el monopolio primaveral de flores!
Los carteles se amotinan
y la lluvia de finas bayonetas
alínea sus primeros escuadrones.

Ventarrón instaura un Orden nuevo
en los paseos
y hace correr a los burgueses
hacia el refugio del aperitivo
en las esquinas reaccionarias.

Las casas se ponen
la escarapela roja del brasero,
y en la ambulancia de las hojas muertas
capitula el buen tiempo.

Boletines de mar y tierra

INDIADA

La garúa del monte
hace chillar las últimas candelas
rotas en resplandores.

Los comuneros llevan la mañana
enredada en los dientes de sus hoces
hacia la tierra baja.

En el vaho de los ponchos serranos
colorados como manzanas
aletean las voces y los pájaros.

BULLETIN OF BAD WEATHER

The northern sky
Raises a black banner
On the barricades of the horizon.

No more sun gold on the banks.
Down with spring's monopoly of flowers!
The handbills mutiny
And fine bayonets of rain
Line up their first squadrons.

Storm wind sets up a new order
In the boulevards
And makes the bourgeoisie run
To seek refuge in aperitives
In reactionary corners.

Houses light
Red cockades of coals.
In the ambulance of the dead leaves
Good weather capitulates.

INDIAN REBELLION

Drizzle from the mountain
Makes the last firewood hiss,
Broken in brilliance.

The communal villagers carry the sunrise
Caught in the teeth of their sickles,
Down to the earth below.

In the steam from the mountain ponchos,
Tinted like apples,
Flutter voices and birds.

Hacia la tierra gorda de gavillas,
en el ala cóncava de los sombreros
baja el viento del páramo.

Los caminos arrieros conducen en la noche
en los carros del aire
racimos de canciones.

La indiada lleva la mañana
en la protesta de sus palas.

Boletines de mar y tierra

DISCURSO ANONIMO

Camaradas: el mundo está construído sobre nuestros
    muertos
y nuestros pies han creado todas las rutas.
Mas, bajo el cielo de todos, no hay un palmo de sombra
para nosotros los que hemos hecho florecer las cúpulas.

El pan, nieto rubio del sembrador, el techo
—fronda de barro y sol que cubre la familia—,
el derecho de amar y de andar, no son nuestros:
Somos los negreros de nuestra propia vida.

La dicha, el mar que no hemos visto nunca,
las ciudades que jamás visitaremos
se alzan en nuestros puños cerrados como frutos
anunciando la más grave cosecha de los tiempos.

¡Sólo el derecho a morir, camaradas del mundo!
Cien manos se reparten las ofrendas del Globo.
Tiempo es ya de lanzarse a las calles y plazas
a rescatar la Obra construída por nosotros.

El tiempo manual

Toward the earth, fat with sheaves,
In the concave brim of the hats
The highland wind comes down.

At night the muleteer roads
Convey bunches of songs
In carts of air.

The Indian rebellion carries the morning
In the protest of its shovels.

ANONYMOUS SPEECH

Comrades: The world is built upon our dead
And our feet have created all the highways.
But, beneath the communal sky there is not a handsbreadth
     of shadow
For us who have made the cupolas blossom.

The bread, red grandson of the sower, the roof—
Foliage of clay and sun that covers the family—
The right to love and to walk, these are not ours:
In our own lives we are slave traders.

Happiness, the sea we have never seen,
The cities we shall never visit
Are held up in our fists, like fruit we clench them,
Announcing the most important harvest of the times.

Only the right to die, world comrades!
A hundred hands divide the offerings of the Globe.
The time has come to fling ourselves into streets and plazas
To redeem the Work which we ourselves constructed.

POEMA HIDROGRAFICO

Los ríos se buscan por el mundo
y alargan en la tierra sus trompetas de vidrio.
Los mapas navegantes coleccionan
las biografías azules de los ríos.

Hidrografía ecuatorial
ilustrada de frutas de la tierra.
Ecuador: en tu aro de color
su pereza de loro dormita Suramérica.

Arboles litorales
cogidos por el lazo de la culebra boba.
Cocotero mulato de cintura flexible.
Bananero de intestinos rosas.

Bosques agujereados por los loros.
Vivienda de caña
del montuvio domador de mosquitos
y degollador de cocos de agua.

Bravos ríos serranos:
Aguas mordientes como espuelas
que hacen encabritar a los caballos.

Garabato infantil del puente
por donde pasa todas las mañanas
una india con un cántaro de leche.

Orillas orientales con pueblos de perdices.
Tortugas de ojos de piedra,
lavaderos de oro
y raíces paralíticas de ciencia.

Arbol de goma
—escalera de los nativos—
parado bajo el cielo con una herida honda.

HYDROGRAPHIC POEM

Rivers seek each other through the world
And spread in the earth their glassy trumpets.
Navigation charts collect
The blue biographies of rivers.

Equatorial hydrography
Illustrated with fruits of the earth.
Ecuador: in your hoop of color
South America dozes in its parrot stupor.

Trees of the shore
Hung with the bow of the silly snake.
Mulatto coconut tree with flexible waist.
Banana tree with rosy entrails.

Forests pierced by the parrots.
Reed hut, home of the shore dweller,
Tamer of mosquitoes
And headsman of the coconuts.

Fierce mountain rivers:
Waters biting like spurs
Which set horses plunging.

Infant pothook of the bridge
Where every morning an Indian woman passes
Carrying milk in a pitcher.

Eastern shores peopled with partridges.
Turtles with eyes of stone,
Gold washings
And paralytic roots of science.

Rubber tree—
Staircase for the natives—
With its deep wound, upright under the sky.

Botes de madera salvaje
donde llevan fusiles y semillas
los rubios inmigrantes.

Corre un rumor de arados
junto a los grandes ríos.
Los colonos descalzos ven doblarse un arco iris
en la tierra peinada de surcos benditos.

Sierra de los ríos labradores,
Litoral de los ríos artesanos,
Oriente de los ríos misioneros:
¡sobre las aguas dulces echemos nuestros barcos!

El tiempo manual

EL EXTRANJERO

Un territorio helado me rodea,
una zona impermeable y silenciosa
donde se apagan los ardientes signos
y su sentido pierden los terrestres idiomas.

Extensiones de plantas y ciudades
que anima solamente la ubicuidad del viento,
latitud abreviada por la noche,
meridianos perdidos en el mapa del sueño.

Ni un gesto de amistad del pájaro o la nube
o el gregario tejado cejijunto.
Un mudo monje verde en cada árbol habita
y un cielo sin pupilas mira el mundo.

Entre rostros cambiantes y edificios que crecen
busco la salvadora compañía,
mas esconde su fruta un hueso amargo
y me queda en las manos su forma de ceniza.

Boats of rough wood
In which blond immigrants
Carry seeds and rifles.

A sound of plows prevails
Close to the great rivers.
Barefoot colonists see a rainbow reflected
In the earth combed with blessed furrows.

Sierra of toiling rivers,
Coast of artisan rivers,
Orient of missionary rivers,
Let us launch our ships on fresh waters!

THE STRANGER

A frozen territory surrounds me,
A zone of impermeability and silence
Where burning signs are extinguished
And earthly idioms lose their meaning.

Extensions of plants and cities
Animated only by the ubiquity of the wind,
Latitude cut short by night,
Meridians lost in the map of sleep.

Not a gesture of friendship offered by bird or cloud
Or the gregarious roof with the meeting eyebrows.
A mute green monk inhabits each tree
And a sky with no pupils stares at the world.

Among changing faces and buildings that grow
I seek the companionship that would save,
But each fruit hides its bitter kernel
And leaves its cindery shape in my hands.

Tú, soledad perdida y recobrada,
entregas a los pájaros tu dominio sin límites
y me interno en tus íntimas provincias
custodiado de fuerzas invisibles.

Sin memoria de brújula ni terrestres idiomas,
espoleado de cielo
vadeando soledades como ríos,
la muda geografía del planeta atravieso.

Biografía para uso de los pájaros (1937)

NADA NOS PERTENECE

Cada día el mismo árbol rodeado
de su verde familia rumorosa.
Cada día el latir de un tiempo niño
que el péndulo mece en la sombra.

El río da sin prisa su naipe transparente.
El silencio camina a un inminente ruido.
Con sus deditos tiernos
la semilla desgarra sus pañales de limo.

Nadie sabe por qué existen los pájaros
ni tu tonel de vino, luna llena,
ni la amapola que se quema viva,
ni la mujer del arpa, dichosa prisionera.

Y hay que vestirse de agua, de dóciles tejidos,
de cosas invisibles y cordiales
y afeitarse con leves despojos de palomas,
de arcoiris y de ángeles.

Y lavar el escaso oro del día
contando sus pepitas cuando el poniente herido
quema todas sus naves y se acerca la noche
capitaneando sus oscuras tribus.

You, solitude lost and recovered,
You surrender your limitless dominion to the birds
And you intern me in your intimate provinces,
Watched over by invisible forces.

Without memory of compass or earthly idioms,
Spurred on by sky,
Wading through solitudes like rivers,
I cross the planet's mute geography.

NOTHING BELONGS TO US

Each day the same tree surrounded
By its murmurous green family.
Each day the beat of an infant rhythm
Which the pendulum rocks in darkness.

The river deals out its transparent card unhurriedly.
Silence travels toward an imminent sound.
The seed with tender fingers
Disengages its swaddlings of mud.

No one knows why the bird exists
Nor your barrel of wine, full moon,
Nor the poppy that burns itself alive,
Nor the woman on the harp, fortunate prisoner.

We must dress in water, in docile fabrics,
In friendly and invisible things.
We must adorn ourselves with trifles cast off by the doves,
The rainbows, and the angels.

And wash the scanty gold of day,
Reckoning its nuggets when the wounded west
Burns all its ships and night approaches
Commanding its dark tribes.

Entonces hablas, Cielo:
Tu alta ciudad nocturna se ilumina.
Tu muchedumbre con antorchas pasa
y en silencio nos mira.

Todas las formas vanas y terrestres:
El joven que cultiva una estatua en su lecho,
la mujer con sus dos corazones de pájaro,
la muerte clandestina disfrazada de insecto.

Cubres toda la tierra, hombre muerto, caído
como una rota jaula
o cascarón quebrado
o vivienda de cal de una monstruosa araña.

Los muertos son los monjes de la Orden
de los anacoretas subterráneos.
¿La muerte es la pobreza suma
o el reino original reconquistado?

Hombre nutrido de años y cuerpos de mujeres:
cuando Dios te espolea te arrodillas
y sólo la memoria de las cosas
pone un calor ya inútil en tus manos vacías.

País secreto (1940)

Then you speak, O sky:
Your tall nocturnal city is lit up.
Your multitudes pass with torches
And silently they stare at us.

All the vain and earthly shapes:
The youth who cherishes a statue in his bed,
The woman with her two bird hearts,
And secret death disguised as an insect.

You cover all the earth, dead man,
Fallen like a broken cage
Or a crumbled shell
Or the limy dwelling of an enormous spider.

The dead are monks of the order
Of subterranean anchorites.
Is death the sum of poverty
Or the original kingdom recovered?

Man, nourished by years and women's bodies,
When God despoils you, you kneel,
And only the memory of things
Sheds a vain warmth on your empty hands.

POLVO, CADAVER DEL TIEMPO

Espíritu de la tierra eres: polvo impalpable.
Omnipresente, ingrávido, cabalgando en el aire
cubres millas marítimas y terrestres distancias
con tu carga de rostros borrados y de larvas.

Oh sutil visitante de las habitaciones.
Los cerrados armarios te conocen.
Despojo innumerable o cadáver del tiempo,
tu ruina se desploma como un perro.

Avaro universal, en huecos y en bodegas
tu oro ligero, inútil, amontonas sin tregua.
Coleccionista vano de huellas y de formas,
les tomas la impresión digital a las hojas.

Sobre muebles y puertas condenadas y esquinas,
sobre pianos, vacíos sombreros y vajillas
tu sombra o mortal ola
extiende su cetrina bandera de victoria.

Sobre la tierra acampas como dueño
con las legiones pálidas de tu imperio disperso.
Oh roedor, tus dientes infinitos devoran
el color, la presencia de las cosas.

Hasta la luz se viste de silencio
con tu envoltura gris, sastre de los espejos.
Heredero final de las cosas difuntas,
todo lo vas guardando en tu ambulante tumba.

País secreto

DUST, CORPSE OF TIME

You are the spirit of earth, impalpable dust.
Omnipresent, impregnated, riding upon the air,
You cover sea miles and terrestrial distances
With your load of fantoms and blurred faces.

O subtle visitor of habitations!
Locked wardrobes know you.
Corpse of time or innumerable plunder,
Your ruin drops to the ground like a dog.

Universal miser, in holes and cellars
Endlessly you pile up your filmy, useless gold.
Vain collector of footsteps and of shapes,
You take the fingerprints of the leaves.

Upon furniture and nailed-up doors and corners,
Upon pianos, empty hats, and tableware,
Your mortal wave or shadow
Extends its yellow banner of victory.

Upon the earth you encamp like a master
With the pale legions of your scattered empire.
O rodent, your infinite teeth devour
The color and shape of everything.

Even the light is dressed in silence
With your gray swaddlings, tailor of mirrors.
Final inheritor of defunct objects,
All shall be stored up in your moving tomb.

I S L A S   S I N   N O M B R E

La canoa que vuelve
con su cosecha de algas
cuenta sobre la arena
su aventura salada,

—bostezo interminable de las ostras—.
Los pinos se conversan,
y por todos sus ojos
espían las cortezas;

mas no ven sino cuervos,
pues éstas son sus islas,
las tierras que escondidos
cadáveres habitan,

donde hay días que reman
sin prisa al horizonte,
y gusanos de luz
que comen caracoles;

ciudades en escombros
sitiadas por sus muertos;
lluvias de verde túnica
sembradoras de insectos,

y pequeñas mujeres
que se nutren de anguilas
o pescados minúsculos
de las tiernas bahías;

donde el tifón desata
sus marítimos potros
los pinos abatiendo y nó el gusano,
cadenilla de polvo;

N A M E L E S S   I S L A N D S

The canoe returning
With its harvest of seaweed
Recounts on the sand
Its salty adventure—

Endless yawn of the oysters.
The pines talk together
And with all its eyes
The bark is watchful;

But sees only the crows
For these are their islands,
The lands which hidden
Corpses dwell in,

Where there are days that row slowly
Toward the horizon
And worms of light
That eat the snails up;

Cities in tatters
Besieged by their dead,
Rains in green gowns
Sowers of insects,

And tiny women
Who are nourished on eels
Or on minnows
From the tender bays;

Where the typhoon unties
Its colts of the sea
Overthrowing the pines, not the worm,
Small chain of dust;

islas donde el silencio
es la más alta dádiva
en la noche de cuero y de pupila
y de ataúd y de alga;

islas sordas de viento,
habitadas de sombras
como un país perdido
en la comarca gris de la memoria.

País secreto

Islands where the silence
Is the loftiest gift
In the night of leather and pupil
And coffin and seaweed;

Wind-deafened islands
Dwelt in by shadows
Like a lost country
In the gray region of memory.

J O S E   G O R O S T I Z A

b. 1901, Vallahermosa, Mexico

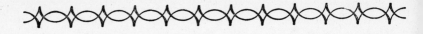

JOSE GOROSTIZA

b. 1901, Vallahermosa, Mexico

GOROSTIZA taught Mexican literature in the National Preparatory School from 1930 to 1931 and general literature in 1933. He is now honorary professor of Spanish American literature in the University of Mexico and consultant to the Mexican Embassy in Havana. He is a delicate and scholarly poet whose early work stems from the seventeenth-century Spanish lyric. In cultivated ballad forms he united a sophisticated symbolism with a simplicity of statement. He has been associated with the *Ulises* group of younger Mexican poets, but while other members of the group have started out as surrealists and passed through various poetic fashions, Gorostiza's poetry has developed steadily and consistently. His second book increases his stature and shows him to be a poet to some extent parallel with Valéry or Rilke. His art is precious, highly refined, and intensely subjective. What gives it its intensity is a certain metaphysical passion which holds together the complicated development of his later poems. Gorostiza represents the tendency on the part of the younger poets of Mexico to retreat from the contemporary scene. Underlying this tendency is a feeling of disorientation and frustration similar to that which, in Anglo-American poetry, we have come to associate with T. S. Eliot. Gorostiza's integrity gives his work its force and his exquisite craftsmanship ranks him as one of the most distinguished contemporary poets of Mexico.

"Iza la flor su enseña" is a section from the book *Muerte sin fin*, which is one long poem, a meditation on death. "¡ Tantan! ¿ Quién es? Es el diablo" is one of the concluding sections of the same poem. The symbol of water runs through the whole book and seems to stand for spiritual grace or the continual flux of life itself. "Preludio" is an example of the extreme complication of his later manner. A whole metaphorical panorama is built up on the concept of the work not spoken by the poet's loved one.

Canciones para cantar en las barcas. Mexico City, 1925.
Muerte sin fin. Mexico City, 1939.

¿QUIEN ME COMPRA UNA NARANJA?

¿Quién me compra una naranja
para mi consolación?
Una naranja madura
en forma de corazón.

La sal del mar en los labios
¡ay de mí!
la sal del mar en las venas
y en los labios recogí.

Nadie me diera los suyos
para besar.
La blanda espiga de un beso
yo no la puedo segar.

Nadie pidiera mi sangre
para beber.
Yo mismo no sé si corre
o si deja de correr.

Como se pierden las barcas
¡ay de mí!
como se pierden las nubes
y las barcas, me perdí.

Y pues nadie me lo pide,
ya no tengo corazón.
¿Quién me compra una naranja
para mi consolación?

Canciones para cantar en las barcas (1925)

WHO WILL BUY ME AN ORANGE?

Who will buy me an orange
Just to console me?
A ripe orange
Shaped like a heart.

The salt of the sea on my lips,
Ah me!
The salt of the sea I gathered
In my veins and upon my lips.

No one would give me hers,
For a kiss.
The delicate stalk of a kiss
Is not for my reaping.

No one would beg my blood
For a drink
And I do not know if it flows
Or if it flows not at all.

Like ships that vanish away,
Ah me!
Like clouds that vanish away
And ships, I was lost.

And since no one seeks it
I still have no heart.
Who will buy me an orange
Just to console me?

PESCADOR DE LUNA

Cuando se mira los faroles rojos
en la orilla del mar,
mi pescador, el de profundos ojos,
pone sus negras redes a pescar.

(El mar ante la noche se ilumina,
y sus olas doradas, al nacer,
florecen como un ansia repentina
en ojos de mujer.)

Pez de luna bruñida no se pesca,
pescador.
Agua del golfo, la ondulada y fresca,
deja que riegue la orilla con amor.

No persigas la forma del lucero,
que ni el agua dormida la dará;
si él, como un sonámbulo viajero,
solo viene y se va.

Que, pobres, las corrientes y la charca
encierran ilusión,
y ajenos al peligro de tu barca
vienen sueños de luz al corazón.

Con los ojos, ya tímidos, escarbas
en los mares rebeldes a cincel,
y puede correr llanto por tus barbas
de serpientes de miel.

El agua misma, la ondulada y fresca,
ponga un poco de sol en tu dolor.
¡Pez de luna bruñida no se pesca,
pescador!

Canciones para cantar en las barcas

FISHERMAN OF THE MOON

When he sees red lanterns
All along the shore,
My fisherman, with eyes of darkness,
Sets his black nets in the sea.

(Before the night the sea is lit up
And its gilded waves at birth
Flower like a sudden longing
In a woman's eyes.)

Fish of burnished moonlight can't be caught,
O fisherman.
Let water from the gulf, so cool and rippled,
Bathe the shore caressingly.

Follow not the bright star's pattern
Which no slumbering wave shall give
If, like a traveler sleepwalking,
It only comes and goes.

Poor lads, for both the pool and currents
Hold illusion
And far from the danger to your vessel
Dreams of light come to your heart.

With your eyes, now timid, you are scraping
Seas rebellious to the chisel,
And the tears may flow along
Honeyed serpents of your beard.

Let the water, cool and rippled,
Set a little sun upon your sorrow.
Fish of burnished moonlight can't be caught,
O fisherman!

PAUSAS II

No canta el grillo. Ritma
la música
de una estrella.

Mide
las pausas luminosas
con su reloj de arena.

Traza
sus órbitas de oro
en la desolación etérea.

La buena gente piensa
—sin embargo—
que canta una cajita
de música en la hierba.

Canciones para cantar en las barcas

OTOÑO

A Jaime Torres Bodet

Un aire frío dispersó la gente,
ramaje de colores.
Mañana es el primer día de otoño.
Los senos quieren iniciar un viaje
de golondrinas en azoro,
y la mirada enfermará de ausencia.

¡Otoño,
todo desnudez de oro!

Pluma de garza contra el horizonte
es la niebla en el alba.
Lo borrará de pronto con un ala

P A U S E S   I I

The cricket does not sing. It ticks out
The music
Of a star.

It measures
The luminous pauses
With its hourglass.

It traces
The golden orbits
In ethereal desolation.

The good citizen thinks—
Notwithstanding—
A little music box is singing
Among the grass blades.

A U T U M N

To Jaime Torres Bodet

A cold air has scattered the people,
A colored branch.
Tomorrow is the first day of autumn.
Breasts wish to begin a journey
Of startled swallows
And the glance shall grow sick with absence.

Autumn,
All nakedness of gold!

The mist in the dawn
Is a stork feather against the horizon.
It shall soon be rubbed out with a distant

lejana;
pero tendré la tarde aclarecida,
aérea, musical de tus preguntas
esas eternas blandas.

¡Otoño,
todo desnudez el oro!

Tu silencio es agudo como un mástil.
Haré de viento orífice.
Y al roce inmaterial de nuestras pausas,
en los atardeceres del otoño,
nunca sabremos si cantaba el mástil
o el viento mismo atardeció sonoro.

¡Otoño,
todo desnudez en oro!

Canciones para cantar en las barcas

IZA LA FLOR SU ENSEÑA

Iza la flor su enseña,
agua, en el prado.
¡Oh, qué mercadería
de olor alado!

¡Oh, qué mercadería
de tenue olor!
¡cómo inflama los aires
con su rubor!

¡Qué anegado de gritos
está el jardín!
"¡Yo, el heliotropo, yo!"
"¿Yo? El jasmín."

Wing;
But I shall have the rinsed-out twilight,
Airy, musical with your questions,
Those soft eternals.

Autumn,
The gold all nakedness!

Your silence is sharp as a mast.
I shall make a goldsmith out of wind.
And in the immaterial friction of our pauses,
In autumn afternoons,
We shall never know if the mast was singing
Or the wind itself sonorously drew toward evening.

Autumn,
All nakedness in gold!

THE BLOOM HOISTS ITS BANNER

The bloom hoists its banner,
Water, in the pasture.
Oh, what a marketing
Of winged fragrance!

Oh, what a marketing
Of delicate odor!
How the breezes
Are inflamed by its blushes!

What a flood of shouting
Makes up the garden!
"I, I the heliotrope!"
"I, the jasmine."

Ay, pero el agua,
ay, si no huele a nada.

Tiene la noche un árbol
con frutos de ámbar;
tiene una tez la tierra,
ay, de esmeraldas.

El tesón de la sangre
anda de rojo;
anda de añil el sueño;
la dicha, de oro.

Tiene el amor feroces
galgos morados;
pero también sus mieses,
también sus pájaros.

Ay, pero el agua,
ay, si no luce a nada.

Sabe a luz, a luz fría,
sí, la manzana.
¡Qué amanecida fruta
tan de mañana!

¡Qué anochecido sabes,
tú, sinsabor!
¡cómo pica en la entraña
tu picaflor!

Sabe la muerte a tierra,
la angustia a hiel.
Este morir a gotas
me sabe a miel.

Ah, but the water,
What if it has no odor!

The night has a tree
With fruits of amber;
Ah, what a complexion
The earth has, of emeralds!

The blood's pertinacity
Goes in scarlet;
Sleep goes in indigo;
Joy goes golden.

Love has ferocious
Hungry purples;
But also its grain fields,
Also its birds.

Ah, but the water,
What if it shines not at all!

The taste of light, of cold light,
Is the taste of the apple.
What fruit of the daybreak
Dawning so early!

How you taste of nightfalls,
You, anxiety!
How your hummingbird
Pecks at our bowels!

Death tastes of earth,
Anguish of bile,
This dying in drops
I taste like honey.

Ay, pero el agua,
ay, si no sabe a nada.

(Baile)

Pobrecilla del agua,
ay, que no tiene nada,
ay, amor, que se ahoga,
ay, en un vaso de agua.

Muerte sin fin (1939)

¡TAN-TAN! ¿QUIEN ES? ES EL DIABLO

¡Tan-Tan! ¿Quién es? Es el Diablo,
es una espesa fatiga,
un ansia de trasponer
estas lindes enemigas,
este morir incesante,
tenaz, esta muerte viva,
¡oh Dios! que te está matando
en tus hechuras estrictas,
en las rosas y en las piedras,
en las estrellas ariscas
y en la carne que se gasta
como una hoguera encendida,
por el canto, por el sueño,
por el color de la vista.

¡Tan-Tan! ¿Quién es? Es el Diablo,
ay, una ciega alegría,
un hambre de consumir
el aire que se respira,
la boca, el ojo, la mano;
estas pungentes cosquillas
de disfrutarnos enteros

Ah, but the water,
What if the water is tasteless!

(Dance)

Poor little thing of water,
Alas, it has nothing,
Alas for love drowning,
Alas, in a glass of water.

W H O   I S   I T ?

Tap-tap! Who is it? It is the Devil,
It is a thick weariness,
A longing to shift
These hostile boundaries,
This incessant, stubborn dying,
This living death
That kills you, O Lord,
In your precise handiwork,
In the roses and in the stones,
In the diffident stars
And in the flesh that is wasted
Like a blazing bonfire
In the song, in the dream,
In the color of sight.

Tap-tap! Who is it? It is the Devil,
Ah, it is a blind joy,
A hunger to consume
The air that we breathe
With the mouth, the eye, the hand;
Those pungent spasms
Of complete enjoyment

en solo un golpe de risa,
ay, esta muerte insultante,
procaz, que nos asesina
a distancia, desde el gusto
que tomamos en morirla,
por una taza de te,
por una apenas caricia.

¡Tan-Tan! ¿Quién es? Es el Diablo,
es una muerte de hormigas
incansables, que pululan
¡oh Dios! sobre tus astillas;
que acaso te han muerto allá,
siglos de edades arriba,
sin advertirlo nosotros,
migajas, borra, cenizas
de ti, que sigues presente
como una estrella mentida
por su sola luz, por una
luz sin estrella, vacía,
que llega al mundo escondiendo
su catástrofe infinita.

(Baile)

Desde mis ojos insomnes
mi muerte me está acechando,
me acecha, sí, me enamora
con su ojo lánguido.
¡Anda, putilla del rubor helado,
anda, vámonos al diablo!

Muerte sin fin

In one burst of laughter,
Ah, this shameless, insulting death
That assassinates us
From a distance
Out of the pleasure
That we take in dying
With a cup of tea,
With a mere caress.

Tap-tap! Who is it? It is the Devil,
It is a death of tireless ants,
That pullulate
Upon the chips of you, O Lord,
For perhaps they have killed you, yonder,
Hundreds of ages before,
Without notifying us,
Crumbs, dregs, ashes of you,
Who are still present
Like a lying star
Only by its light, by an empty
Light without star
That reaches the world, hiding
Its infinite catastrophe.

(Dance)

Out of my sleepless eyes
My death is spying upon me,
It spies upon me, indeed, it charms me
With its languid eye.
Come, little whore with the frozen blush,
Come, let us go to the devil!

PRELUDIO

"Empecemos por invocar en nuestro canto a las Musas
Helicónides."   Hesíodo, *Teogonía*.

Esa palabra que jamás asoma
a tu idioma cantado de preguntas,
ésa, desfalleciente,
que se hiela en el aire de tu voz,
sí, como una respiración de flautas
contra un aire de vidrio evaporada,
¡mírala, ay, tócala!
¡mírala, ahora!
en esta exangüe bruma de magnolias,
en esta nimia floración de vaho
que—ensombrecido en luz el ojo agónico,
y a funestos pestillos
anclado el tenue ruido de las alas—
guarda un ángel de sueño en la ventana.
¡Qué muros de cristal, amor, qué muros!
¿ay, para qué silencios de agua?

Esa palabra, sí, esa palabra
que se coagula en la garganta
como un grito de ámbar,
¡mírala, ay, tócala!
¡mírala, ahora!
Mira que, noche a noche, decantada
en el filtro de un áspero silencio,
quedóse a tanto enmudecer desnuda,
hiriente e inequívoca
—así en la entraña de un reloj la muerte,
así la claridad en una cifra—
para gestar este lenguaje nuestro,
inaudible,
que se abre al tacto insomne

P R E L U D E

"Let us begin by invoking the Muses of Helicon in our
    song."   Hesiod, *Theogony*.

That word which never appears
In your singing, questioning speech,
The one which languishes,
Which freezes in the air of your voice,
Yes, like a breathing of flutes,
Into evaporated air of glass,
Look at it, ah, touch it!
Look at it, now!
In this bloodless mist of magnolias,
In this prolix flowering of vapor
Which keeps an angel of sleep in the window—
The agonic eye darkened in light
And by dismal locks,
The thin sound of wings anchored.
What walls of crystal, O love, what walls,
Ah, for what silences of water?

That word, yes, that word
Which thickens in the throat
Like an amber shriek,
Look at it, ah, touch it!
Look at it, now!
See how, night after night, decanted
Through the filter of a sharp silence,
It diminishes by so much to grow silent, naked,
Whetted and unequivocal
As death in the works of a watch,
As the clarity in a cipher,
To produce this language of ours,
Inaudible,
Which opens to the sleepless touch

en la arena, en el pájaro, en la nube,
cuando negro de oráculos retruena
el panorama de la profecía.

¿Quién, si ella no,
pudo fraguar este universo insigne
que nace como un héroe en tu boca?
¡mírala, ay, tócala!
¡mírala, ahora,
incendiada en un eco de nenúfares!
¿No aquí su angustia asume la inocencia
de una hueca retórica de lianas?
Aquí, entre líquenes de orfebrería
que arrancan de minúsculos canales,
¿no echó a tañer al aire
sus cándidas mariposas de escarcha?
Qué, en lugar de esa fe que la consume
hasta la transparencia del destino,
¿no aquí—escapada al dardo
tenaz de la estatura—
se remonta insensata una palmera
para estallar en su ficción de cielo,
maestra en fuegos no,
mas en puros deleites de artificios?

Esa palabra, sí, esa palabra,
ésa desfalleciente,
que se ahoga en el humo de una sombra,
ésa que gira—como un soplo—cauta
sobre bisagras de secreta lama,
ésa en que el aura de la voz se astilla,
desalentada
como si rebotara
en una bella úlcera de plata,
ésa que baña sus vocales ácidas
en la espuma de las palomas sacrificadas,
ésa que se congela de la fiebre

In the sand, in the bird, in the cloud,
When, black with oracles, it thunders
In the panorama of prophecy.

What, if not this,
Could forge this frail universe
Which is born like a hero in your mouth?
Look at it, ah, touch it!
Look at it, now,
Set on fire in an echo of white water lilies!
Does not its anguish assume here the innocence
Of an empty rhetoric of lianas?
Here, among silverwork lichens
That issue from minute canals,
Has it not flung its snowy butterflies of frost
Into the air to play?
Indeed, in place of this faith that consumes it
Even to the transparency of destiny—
Having escaped into the stubborn
Dart of its height
Does not a palm tree soar up insensately here
To burst in its fictive sky,
Adept not in gunnery
But in the pure delights of fireworks?

That word, yes, that word,
The one which swoons,
Which chokes in the smoke of a shadow,
The one which whirls—like a puff—warily
Above hinges of secret slime,
The one on which the aura of your voice is splintered,
Deprived of breath
As if it rebounded in a beautiful silver ulcer,
The one that bathes its acid vowels
In the foam of sacrificed doves,
The one which congeals from fever

cuando no, ensimismada, se calcina
en la brusca intemperie de una lágrima,
¡mírala, ay, tócala!
¡mírala, ahora!
¡mírala, ausente toda de palabra,
sin voz, sin eco, sin idioma, exacta,
mírala cómo traza
en muros de cristal amores de agua!

Poemas no coleccionados

When it does not calcify pensively
In the brusque open air of a tear,
Look at it, touch it!
Look at it, now,
Look at it, entirely empty of word,
Without voice, without echo, without speech, precise,
See how it traces
Love made of water on walls of crystal!

PABLO DE ROKHA

(CARLOS DIAZ LOYOLA)

b. 1894, Licantén, Chile

PABLO DE ROKHA
(CARLOS DIAZ LOYOLA)
b. 1894, Licantén, Chile

PABLO DE ROKHA is something of a storm center in Chilean poetry. He edits his own review, *Multitud,* in which he battles for his literary and political views. He has been at various times salesman, editor, teacher in the University of Chile, and unsuccessful candidate for the Chamber of Deputies of Santiago de Chile. He has seven children, the eldest of whom, Carlos, is already a promising poet. Rokha's poetry is violently experimental, many of the early volumes being written in "dynamic prose"; and one poem, "Suramérica," has been the subject of a controversy as to its relation to the work of Joyce. He has absorbed such diverse influences as Lautréamont, Marx, Freud, and Blake. Out of a fantastic and undisciplined imagery he creates a heroic emotion. At times he attacks the reactionary elements in society, at times he celebrates the power of the proletariat. Concerning poetry, he says, "The people's voice of the bards does not foretell, testify, or prophesy, it *builds* worlds beloved by the great genesis—it does not create outside of things, it *is*, it is what it creates . . ." He therefore considers himself to be the expression of the subconscious of the masses.

"Canto de tribu" reveals Rokha's Freudian approach to economic determinism; there he traces the struggle for human progress in terms of primitive instincts and identifies the energy of rebellion with the sexual drive. His method is interesting, despite its structural confusion, because it represents an attempt similar to that of the surrealists to create new myths. In this he is unique among marxist poets since, in most cases, social inspiration has been expressed in rather journalistic terms. Such symbols as the sword, the serpent, and the apple run through all his later poems and denote general qualities, a device also used by Neruda. In fact, although their points of view are widely divergent, Pablo de Rokha, Huidobro, and Neruda technically have much in common. In "Los días y las noches subterráneas" the apostrophe is to his wife, Winett, also a poet, who assists him in editing *Multitud*.

Los gemidos. Santiago de Chile, 1922.
U. Santiago de Chile, 1927.
Suramérica. Santiago de Chile, 1927.
Satanás. Santiago de Chile, 1927.
Heroísmo sin alegría (essays). Santiago de Chile, 1927.
Ecuación (aesthetic theory). Santiago de Chile, 1929.
Escritura de Raimundo Contreras. Santiago de Chile, 1929.
Jesucristo. Santiago de Chile, 1930.
Canto de trinchera. Santiago de Chile, 1933.
Gran temperatura. Santiago de Chile, 1937.
Morfología del espanto. Santiago de Chile, 1942.

L O S   P U E B L O S   M A R I N O S

Floridos de redes triviales, llenos de pupilas, llenos de
pupilas verdes y gente robusta, los pueblos marinos sueñan,
sueñan, sueñan fumando la pipa añeja de las brumas sobre
los acantilados rotundos, sobre los acantilados rotundos y
las costas tranquilas, modestas, calladas y medicinales.

¡Cuán lejanos están de la vida, cuán lejanos! . . . la tonada
monumental de las olas continuas, continuas, continuas y
múltiples, llena de ruïdos grandes su actitud . . . caracoles,
caracoles sonoros como pianos gigantes, caracoles sonoros
como pianos gigantes . . .

Pegados a las rocas egregias como templos, como niños,
como cantos, agarrados, agarrados como moluscos agarrados
a la energía, a la energía permanente de las piedras, los
pueblos marinos cantan los pueblos marinos, los cánticos del
horizonte, las tardes augustas, las aves inquietas, las albas,
la novela de los marineros y los barcos trágicos, los romanti-
cismos de la niña, la esposa y los pañuelos lo mismo que
errantes alas que uniesen las tierras y el mar! . . .

Gestos de países, gestos de países desconocidos, són de
viajes tienen los pueblos marinos . . .

Los gemidos (1922)

SEAFARING TOWNS

Flowering with trivial nets, full of pupils, full of green pupils and robust people, seaside towns dream, dream, dream, smoking the musty pipe of the fogs over the rounded steeps, over the rounded steeps and quiet coasts, modest, silent, and medicinal.

How far they are from life, how far! . . . the monumental tune of continuous waves, continuous, continuous, continuous and multiple, its posture full of huge noises . . . snails, snails sonorous as gigantic pianos, snails sonorous as gigantic pianos . . .

Fastened to the rocks, eminent as temples, like children, like songs, clutching, clutching like mollusks, clutching at the energy, at the permanent energy of the stones, seaside towns sing seaside towns, chants of the horizon, august evenings, inquiet birds, dawns, the novel of sailors and tragic ships, the romanticisms of the little girl, the wife, and handkerchiefs like wandering wings that unite the lands and the sea! . . .

Faces of countries, faces of unknown countries, sound of voyages belong to seaside towns . . .

TRENO

Cansancio de los huesos
y el corazón, ¡cansancio! . . .
cansancio torvo y negro,
definitivo y ácido . . .

Fatiga de las piernas,
fatiga de los mundos,
fatiga de la lengua,
las cosas y los frutos . . .

Andar, andar rodando
como un carretón viejo
por los caminos largos . . .
¡cansancio de los huesos! . . .

Los gemidos

LOS PALIDOS CONQUISTADORES

Caracteres épicos, caracteres épicos, ejecutivos o rotundos,
rotundos, rotundos, y almas de bronce, acero, piedra, huesos
aporreados, carnes endurecidas, hombres del hablar conciso,
enérgico, sencillo, auténtico, autoritario, exacto, y la acción
roja, roja ardiendo a priori, anacoretas-espadachines, espada-
chines-anacoretas, aventureros a quienes el hambre y la sed
de oro, la gloria, las hazañas—la gloria!, la gloria!—trasmu-
taron de farsantes en héroes, de farsantes en héroes, a fuerza
de tener el alma hirviendo, a fuerza de tener el alma hir-
viendo, a fuerza de tener el alma hirviendo a setenta y un
grados a la sombra.

Oscuros, analfabetos, ignorantes soldados ignorantes, tra-
zásteis el polígono de las inmensas urbes contemporáneas y

LAMENT

Weariness of the bones
And of the heart, weariness! . . .
Twisted and black weariness,
Acid and definite . . .

Tiredness of the legs,
Tiredness of worlds,
Tiredness of the tongue
And of fruits and things . . .

To go, to go round and round
Like an old cart
Over long roadways . . .
Weariness of the bones! . . .

THE PALE CONQUERORS

Epic characters, epic characters, executive or rounded, rounded, rounded, and souls of bronze, steel, stone, tempered bones, hardened flesh, men of concise speech, energetic, simple, authentic, authoritative, exact, and red, red action, blazing a priori, anchorite-duelists, duelist-anchorites, adventurers whom hunger and thirst for gold, glory, exploits— glory! glory!—transformed from clowns into heroes, from clowns into heroes by virtue of having souls boiling, by virtue of having souls boiling, by virtue of having souls boiling at a hundred degrees in the shade.

Obscure, illiterate, ignorant, ignorant soldiers, you traced out the polygons of immense contemporary cities and were fuisteis los primeros pobladores sobre la parda, parda tierra parda, parda, humilde, agrícola, ruborizándose como mujer á la cual sorprendiéramos desnuda; voluntades con el yatagán desenvainado, perseguíais dos destinos: morir colgados á la horca o coronados de laureles.

Y, os llamáseis Pedro de Valdivia, Hernán Cortés o Francisco Pizarro, Napoleón, érais lo mismo: valientes, borrachos, canallas, dementes o locos geniales, contradictorios, atrabiliarios, es decir, instrumentos irresponsables del dinamismo cósmico y las nocturnas fuerzas de la vida; conquistadores, os saludo porque teníais mucho de quijotes-poetas-caudillos cruzando las setecientas fatigas del horizonte con vuestros absurdos, pintarrajeados, metafóricos trajes y la sonora actitud novelesca, colmados de ilusiones, ambiciones, emociones heroicas, descomunales, llenos de paisajes los ojos, dormidos á la sombra de un gran sueño distante y ancho cual los cielos, y con diez céntimos, y con diez céntimos en los bolsillos!

Los gemidos

CANTO DE TRIBU

Patagua del milenario,
a cuya influencia descanso y escribo la lengua eterna,
como los racimos de barro
encadenamiento de raíces resplandecientes,
vivienda de cuero.

Unidad familiar, herida,
"bodega de frutos del país," tinaja de instintos,
paloma de sol y pan.

En lagares de piel de buey, brama el vino de los antepasados,
hoy, nosotros, con el puñal entre los dientes,
peleamos contra los cementerios, rodeados de sepulturas y
osamentas, a toda historia,

the first populators of the dusky dusky earth, dusky, dusky, humble, agricultural, blushing like a woman whom we have caught naked, wills with daggers unsheathed, you pursued two destinies: to die hanging from the gallows or crowned with laurels.

And, whether you were called Pedro de Valdivia, Hernán Cortés, Francisco Pizarro or Napoleon, you were the same: brave men, drunkards, ruffians, lunatics or mad geniuses, contradictory, irascible, which is to say irresponsible instruments of cosmic dynamism and the nocturnal forces of life; conquerors, I salute you for you possessed much of quixotes-poets-leaders, crossing the seven-hundred fatigues of the horizon with your absurd, bedaubed, metaphorical clothes and the sonorous gesture of fiction, heaped with illusions, ambitions, heroic enormous emotions, eyes full of landscapes, sleeping in the shadow of a great distant dream, broad as the skies and with ten cents, and with ten cents in your pockets!

TRIBAL LAY

Linden of the millennium
Under whose influence I rest and write the eternal language,
Like lumps of clay
Linkage of gleaming roots,
Habitation of leather.

Wounded domestic unity,
"Storehouse of fruits of the country," earthern jar of instincts,
Pigeon of sun and bread.

In wine presses of oxhide the wine of our ancestors bellows.
And we, today, with the dagger between our teeth,
Battle with cemeteries, surrounded with sepulchers and
skeletons, throughout history,

encadenados a la antigüedad húmeda,
buscando lo humano en los subterráneos, entre chacales,
    entre águilas, entre leones y tribus guerreras,
ansiosos de supervivencia, como plantas, como animales,
    como cosas,
repletos de esa vida bruta, que relampaguea en las botellas
    y aquel resplandor de divinidad en lo eterno del pie
    femenino.

Contra las fogatas edificadas más allá de los péndulos,
arden las danzas y el alarido y los llantos,
al crepitar de las encinas desenganchadas, con viento in-
    menso, quemando nidos, quemando huevos de cóndores,
y nosotros nos encadenamos a la patriarcal aurora.

En prehistoria, en especie, en documento de médula, re-
    lampagueando,
en raíz, en verdad, en canción nos definimos,
desnudos de huesos y de actos, de sangre brillante y aterra-
    dora,
siendo la substancia del mundo,
su actitud proletaria, hambre de clase, su poderosa y asom-
    brada juventud, el ímpetu como de águila,
siendo sociedad pura y tremenda,
cadena, expresión, polea de rodaje indescriptible,
clan auroral, con inmensos ojos de uva,
risa de materia, hoja de substancia, en proceder de abejorros,
los mostos eternos y su pantalón de barro,
danza de vientres, de palomas, de flores que asumen elemen-
    tales vellos de sexo,
castaña de toro, asada en el subconsciente,
leyenda de cuchilla, rey de costumbre, saco de mundo de
    dios de sueño.

El ademán emerge, pues, desde cuando adoraba astros el
    hombre,
y, adentro de nosotros aúlla el chivato, el orangután, el

Locked in moist antiquity,
Seeking the human, underground, among jackals, among
 eagles, among lions and warlike tribes,
Eager to survive, like plants, like animals, like things,
Full of that brute life that sparkles in bottles and that divine
 splendor in the eternity of a woman's foot.

Against bonfires built higher than pendulums,
Burn the dances and the scream and the tears,
In the crackling of uprooted oaks overthrown by immense
 wind, burning nests, burning condor's eggs,
And we chain ourselves to the patriarchal dawn.

In prehistory, in the species, in the documents of the spinal
 cord,
Shining, in the root, in truth, in song, we define ourselves,
Naked of bone and actions, brilliant and terrible with blood,
Being the substance of the world,
Its proletarian attitude, class hunger, its powerful and aston-
 ishing youth and eagle's impetuosity,
Being society, tremendous and pure,
Chain, expression, pulley with an indescribable wheel,
Dawn clan with immense eyes like grapes,
Laughter of matter, leaf of substance, in the behavior of
 bees,
The eternal juices of the grape in its breech of clay,
Dance of bellies, of doves, of flowers which assume the ele-
 mental pubescence of sex,
Bull's chestnut, roasted in the subconscious,
Legend of knife, king of custom, sackful of world of the god
 of sleep.

The gesture emerges from when men worshiped stars,
And within us howls the kid, the orangutan, the goat, male

cabrío, macho entre machos, la bestia astuta y su har-
tura, su lujuria, su bravura,
el carnívoro—ferocidad y eternidad y cráneos,—
o llorando en la lengua obscena el sacerdote inconmensura-
ble.

Sí, en ardientes camas de estiércol,
sembrando los mitos del amor, lo sagrado y lo esplendoroso,
flor del clítoris, el dios vaginal que llamea,
paloma del himeneo, toda roja y como madura de valores,
a tal manera de misterio nos sumamos,
o enamorando en colchones de llamas la materia, reducién-
dola a expresión pura,
incendiándola, sublimándola en el yo social y su enigma.

Gran temperatura (1937)

ELEGIA DE TODOS
LOS TIEMPOS

Camino, ruta, sendero, callejón de soledad, con esbirros,
embanderado de mujeres y de ciudades, por océanos, o árbol
trágico y matemático, a aquella gran ribera desesperada,
vía de luto, calle de dolores, senda de llanto,
gran vereda asoleada y floreal como trigo, como montaña,
como pecho de serpiente, lago de oro, dios enloquecido,
todos van hacia la misma orilla . . .

Allí donde están tendidos los muertos y los recuerdos de los
muertos,
y la desgracia humana se reúne y se azota y se precipita y se
abruma contra el oleaje irremediable, como una gran
vaca idiota,
porque, de un gran amor, de un gran amor, sólo quedan los
sexos vacíos.

Azotado o poderoso, humillado o altanero, alegre como el
vino o la mujer desnuda,

among males, the clever beast and its satiety, its lechery,
its bravery,
The carnivore—ferocity and eternity and skulls—
Or the immeasurable priest weeping in the obscene lan-
guage.

Yes, in burning beds of dung,
Sowing the myths of love, the sacred and splendid,
Flower of the clitoris, the flaming vaginal god,
Hymeneal dove, all red and as if ripe with values,
In such mysterious way we are summed up,
Or adoring matter on mattresses of flames, reducing it to its
pure expression,
Kindling it, sublimating it in the social I and its engima.

ELEGY FOR ALL AGES

Road, route, footpath, alley of solitude with its myrmidons,
Adorned with women and cities, beside oceans, or tragic and
mathematical tree by this same great despairing beach,
Roadway of mourning, street of sorrows, pathway of tears,
Great sunny lane blooming like wheat field, like mountain,
like breast of serpent, like lake of gold, like crazed god,
All go toward the same shore . . .

Yonder, where the dead are stretched out and the memory
of the dead
And human affliction collects and scourges itself and throws
itself and wears itself out against the irremediable surf
like a great idiotic cow,
Since after a great love, after a great love, only spent sexes
remain.

Scourged or powerful, humiliated or exalted, gay as wine or
a woman naked,

triste y grande, como la caída del sol, profundo
como la unidad y sus misterios, como la voz que emerge,
　　desde la especie, por debajo del hombre enorme.

Lenin o Jesús, las grandes banderas,
el hambriento, el rico, el enfermo, el que tenía una sola flor,
　　y se la robaron,
y el amo de la propiedad atrabiliaria,
éstos, aquéllos, ésos, a la muerte desesperados, irán cayendo,
　　irán cayendo, irán cayendo, despavoridos,
aunque se agarren a la humanidad, que se derrumba y se
　　desploma con ellos,
o con nosotros, con todos nosotros,
como un carro de cosechas, en la quebrada cordillerana.

Sí, el ser perece, pero, por adentro de la historia, naciendo y
　　muriendo heroicamente,
todo y sólo lo humano, enarbolado de trabajadores, sobrevive
　　y resplandece, encima de la gran tiniebla,
la sociedad, coronada de obreros.

Eternamente, las masas humanas son lo eterno, individuo-
　　universo-infinito,
en multitud orgánica y dramática,
condensados, estructurados, sumados, soviéticamente en
　　enormes soviets de voces.

Muere el hombre no tronchando nunca la cadena,
la cadena encadenada, de fuego y hierro del suceder eco-
　　nómico,
porque, tiempo y mundo son lo mismo;
astros de angustia, manzanas de sueños, naranjas de miedo,
　　vientre de flor celeste,
y en los cementerios culmina la vida.

Apretándose y destrozándose, hacia la muralla enlutada,

Sad and huge as a sunset, profound
As unity and its mysteries, like the voice that arises from the
    species from beneath the immense man.

Lenin or Jesus, great banners,
The hungry, the rich, the sick, he who had but a single
    flower and they stole it from him,
And the owner of black bilious property,
Those others, the ones who, despairing unto death will go
    falling, will go falling, will go falling in terror,
Even though they cling to humanity that collapses and crum-
    bles
With them or with us, with all of us,
Like a cart full of produce in the mountain pass.

Yes, existence perishes but inside of history, being born and
    dying heroically,
Everything and only what is human, hung about with
    laborers, survives and flourishes on top of the great
    darkness,
The society crowned with workers.

Eternally, the human masses are the eternal, individual-
    universal-infinite,
In organic and dramatic multitude,
Close packed, constructed, summed up, sovietically, in enor-
    mous soviets of voices.

Man dies, never cutting the chain,
The chain linked of fire and iron of economic determinism,
Since time and the world are the same;
Stars of anguish, apples of dreams, oranges of fear, belly of
    celestial bloom,
And life reaches its culmination in cemeteries.

Crushing itself and shattering itself toward the wall in
    mourning,

agachado el proletario, bajo los látigos del explotador, que
restalla la huasca ensangrentada y difícil,
como una inmensa copa de salud, empuña la dialéctica.

Gran temperatura

LOS DIAS Y LAS NOCHES SUBTERRANEAS

Como a una espalda de años, la azota la cadena del mar,
    y ruge
cuando la gran águila roja, por la cual caminan todos los
    muertos del mundo cavando sus sepulturas, estremece
    el atardecer ululante
mi palabra de sol, sentada como montaña.

Tú, entre navíos y fusiles,
desnuda como un puñal de oro, con solo un ojo en la cabeza
    de plata santa
con la lengua untada de miel y chirimoyas,
expandiendo el maíz y el frejol y las chichas y las fogatas y
    las hojas de Marzo,
rodeada de maderas y gallinas y flores y buques y reyes
sentados en el funeral de piedra, a la puerta de los pueblos
    antiguos, comerciantes en aceite,
con tus tres retratos en la cara.

Ganados y canastos, la gran azúcar negra del crepúsculo,
de donde emergen los cuervos, estrellándose contra los
    cementerios subterráneos, contra los cráneos de Dios en
    la tiniebla,
y adentro del cual las azucenas paren lagartijas,
o pescados de sangre y de muerte, llenos de lluvia, como los
    castaños del Sur de Francia,
o estrellas de vidrio o palomas o la agricultura . . .

Sí, naciente, relampagueante, surgente,
a la manera de las pataguas llenas de torcazas del año

The proletariat, bowed down under the lashes of the ex-
    ploiter who cracks the bloody and difficult whip,
As though drinking a huge toast, dialectics raises in its fist.

SUBTERRANEAN DAYS
AND NIGHTS

The chain of the sea roars and lashes it as if it were a back
    made of years,
When the great red eagle by which all the dead of the world
    travel, digging their graves, stirs the howling twilight,
My word of sun, planted like a mountain.

You, among ships and guns,
Naked as a dagger of gold, like a single eye in a sacred silver
    head,
Like the tongue anointed with honey and cherimoyas,*
Unfolding corn, beans, corn whisky and the bonfires and the
    leaves of March,
Surrounded with wood and fowls and flowers and boats and
    kings
Seated on stony funerals, at the gate of ancient towns,
    dealers in oil,
And your three portraits in one face.

Cattle and baskets, the great black sugar of twilight
From which crows emerge, crashing against underground
    cemeteries, against the skulls of God in the dark,
And within which white lilies bear lizards,
Or fishes of blood and death, full of rain like chestnut trees
    in southern France,
Or glass stars or pigeons or husbandry . . .

Yes, nascent, glittering, sprouting,
In the manner of lindens full of the year's wood pigeons

* The cherimoya is a South American fruit similar to the custard apple.

y también religión en los viñedos,
cubres mis poemas, la cuchilla social, el amor, la tinaja
    eclesiástica, en donde arde y ruge el vino,
poderosa Winett estrellada por el grito del cielo,
clamante, como un álamo trágico, a la entrada de la estación
    caída,
viajera de los abandonados pueblos y los cortijos,
en los que murieron los dueños, y todo es pasado, antepasado,
    pretérito, como el último lanchón de las bahías,
y llegas, cantando la tonada matemática de las cántaras,
toda de humo, fina, sin tiempo, guinda de aquellas huertas
    inmensas que engendran la primavera.

Sobre algas fuertes, como sexos o coyunturas,
y árboles submarinos, cargados de moluscos y pescados y
    patos y santos y canarios de océano,
gravita tu cabello adolescente.

Un caballo mineral galopa la historia,
y ha anclado un gran navío en tus pupilas, un gran navío
    empavezado de banderas corsarias;
soy como forjado a cuchilla,
hecho a balazos o hachazos, con la herramienta de piedras
    de las cavernas,
con el combo de los herreros,
con el puñal de los que afrontaron la suerte y la muerte,
    cruzados por el cinturón de los héroes,
con la voluntad afilada del cazador de tiburones o de ele-
    fantes,
con la mochila del espía y el pecho de hierro y cruces del
    soldado y del pirata,
con el elemento colosal del panfletario,
del orador de masas, del político dramático, que tiene un
    dedo de fuego,
con la espada del alacrán, clavada
en las entrañas de Dios, como un corazón colorado,
o una gran idea,

And likewise religion in vineyards,
You cover my poems, knife of society, love, the ecclesiastical
 jar in which the wine burns and roars,
Mighty Winett, shattered by the shriek of the sky,
Clamoring like a tragic elm at the entrance of a tumbledown
 station,
Traveler in abandoned towns, in farmhouses
Where the owners have died and all is past, long past, pret-
 erit, like the last barge in the bays,
And you come singing the mathematical tune of milk cans,
Entirely smoke, refined, timeless, mazard cherry† of those
 immense garden plots that engender spring.

Your adolescent hair rests upon strong seaweeds like sexes or
 joints
And submarine trees laden with mollusks and fish and ducks
 and saints and ocean canaries.

A mineral horse galops history
And has anchored a great ship in your pupils, a great ship
 adorned with corsair's flags;
I am as if carved by a knife,
Made by bullets or axes by the stone tools of the caves,
By the blacksmith's hammer,
By the dagger of those who confront fate and death girded
 with the belt of heroes,
By the whetted will of the hunter of sharks and elephants,
By the knapsack of the spy and the breast of iron and crosses
 of the soldier and pirate,
By the huge ingredient of the pamphleteer,
By the orator of the masses, the dramatic politician who has
 a finger of fire,
By the sword of the scorpion, fastened
In the bowels of God, like a ruddy heart
Or a great idea,

 † The guinda or mazard cherry is a wild cherry that grows in South Amer-
ica.

con las plumas de los recuerdos extranjeros,
con el león de ceniza, que está rugiendo en la soledad de las
    culturas,
con el gaznate de los asesinos,
con el canto enorme y augural de los carreteros, de los
    arrieros, de los palanqueros de la aurora . . .

Aquí el chacal de los presidiarios siberianos, aúlla,
el toro del Sinaí, la lepra judía y el estercolero de diamante,
las tetas hinchadas de sol entre los cuernos de Dyonisos,
el desierto de asfalto sin ruedas, fruta de goma regia y vien-
    tres de serpiente o ídolo o ébano,
el tambor de cuero de muerto de los guerreros del occidente,
el veneno renacentista, en la azucena de esmeralda y ópalo
    de las marquesas que arden perfume y sexo,
y el tam-tam oscuro y precolombino.

Palparás las entrañas del cielo y del mundo,
oirás su grito de piedra, cortado y desventurado, sin lá-
    grimas,
porque el hombre creó el dolor y el sueño,
sentirás como te crece, entonces, un gran árbol infinito y
    amarillo en medio de la lengua,
cómo Tamerlán y Lenin te saludan desde la muerte,
y como tú comprendes por qué el héroe bolquevique es im-
    prescindible para, en carne y sangre entrar a la historia,
    entendíendola,
cómo se refieren el mundo, el sol, el trigo, en el pan coti-
    diano . . .

Con sólo andando el Gran Poema en el vértice de vértices
    irás distribuyéndote,
haciéndote cosas y sombras y espíritu,
tú, que eres una canción pura, de diamantes y finos puñales,
tú, que empuñas la bayoneta florecida del himno,
tú, que vienes, siempre, desde el orígen de los números, entre
    terribles pieles de víbora,

By the feathers of alien memories,
By the lion of ashes that is roaring in the solitudes of cultures,
By the gullet of assassins,
By the enormous prophetic song of teamsters, of muleteers,
    of brakemen of dawn . . .

Here the jackal of Siberian prisoners, it howls,
The bull of Sinai, the Jewish leprosy, the diamond dung-cart
    driver,
The teats, swollen with sun, between the horns of Dionysus,
The asphalt desert without wheels, fruit of royal rubber and
    serpents' bellies or idols or ebony,
The drum of leather of dead Eastern warriors,
The renaissance poison, the emerald lily, and the opal of the
    marchionesses that burns perfume and sex,
The obscure and pre-Columbian tom-tom.

You shall touch the bowels of the earth and the sky,
You shall hear its stony cry, abrupt and sad, without tears,
Since man created both sorrow and dream,
You shall feel how a great yellow infinite tree grows then in
    the middle of the tongue,
How Tamerlane and Lenin salute you from death,
And as you understand why the Bolshevik hero is indispen-
    sable in order to enter history in flesh and blood, under-
    standing it,
How the world, the sun, the wheat are related to each other
    in our daily bread . . .

By only walking the Great Poem in the vertex of vertices,
    you shall go distributing yourself,
Making yourself objects and shadow and spirit,
You, who are a pure song of diamonds and sharp daggers,
You, who clasp the flowering bayonet of the hymn,
You, who always come from the origin of numbers, among
    terrible viper skins,

y estás en la libertad crucificada,
bajo el signo social de la hoz y el martillo . . .

Guitarras sin figura, como pájaros viudos,
cantan en las almenas, en las murallas de la edad del tiempo,
y el sol ruge como un toro.

Morfología del espanto (1942)

And are crucified in liberty
Beneath the signal to society of the hammer and sickle . . .

Guitars without form, like widowed birds,
Sing in the battlements, in the walls of the epoch of time,
And the sun bellows like a bull.

NICOLAS GUILLEN

b. 1904, Camaguëy, Cuba

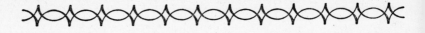

NICOLAS GUILLEN

b. 1904, Camagüey, Cuba

GUILLEN is the leader and most important poet of the Afro-Cuban school, and himself a mulatto. He started to study law in the University of Havana but did not complete the course. Instead, he has been active as an editor, lecturer, and radio speaker. When he ran unsuccessfully for mayor of his native town in 1939, the excellent showing he made was a tribute to his wide popularity. Some of his earlier poetry shows the influence of Villon and Baudelaire; and through all his work runs a bitter strain of social protest and social satire. He has steeped himself in Negro folklore and in the contemporary dance rhythms of Cuba, shaping popular ballads and *sones* into poetry at once simple and serious in intention. These songs are proletarian poetry in the best sense—a vivid interpretation of the life of the people. Guillén's work has great significance in giving artistic form to the contribution of the Negroes and mulattoes to the culture of Latin America. It has also acted as a stimulus to members of the Negro race all through the Caribbean. Guillén visited France and Spain during the Spanish War and also spent some time in Mexico. During this period he wrote poems on anti-Fascist themes. In his last book he departs somewhat from Afro-Cuban inspiration and writes ballads which are closer to the modern Spanish school. His popular songs are the best known portion of his work and some of them have been set to music.

"Mulata" and "Negro bembón" are popular songs bearing a certain relation to American blues. They are both examples of the *son*. "Charity" in "Negro bembón" is the Negro mistress of the subject of the poem. "Sensemayá" is an adaptation of a traditional magical incantation to protect a man killing a snake. The African refrain words are used for their sound value, a typical Afro-Cuban device. Most of these words have already lost their meaning for the modern Cuban and live on in popular tradition as the nonsense refrains of some game songs do in English. *Mayombé,* however refers to a native of a region of the French Congo of the same name. "Diana" is an example of Guillén's recent Spanish ballad style.

Motivos de són. Havana, 1930.
Sóngoro cosongo. Havana, 1931.
West Indies Ltd. Havana, 1934.
España. Havana, 1937.
Cantos para soldados y sones para turistas. Mexico City, 1937.
Sóngoro cosongo y otros poemas (selection from earlier books and additional new poems). Havana, 1943.

MULATA

Ya yo me enteré, mulata,
mulata, ya sé que me dise
que yo tengo la narise
como nudo de cobbata.

Y fíjate bien que tú
no ere tan adelantá,
poqque tu boca e bien grande
y tu pasa, colorá.

Tanto tren con tu cueppo,
tanto tren;
tanto tren con tu boca,
tanto tren;
tanto tren con tu sojo,
tanto tren;

Si tú supiera, mulata,
la beddá:
que yo con mi negra tengo
y no te quiero pa na.

Sóngoro cosongo (1931)

YELLOW   GIRL

I know what you're saying, yellow girl,
I know it ain't no lie.
I got a nose on my face
As big as a knot on a tie.

I don't see where you got yourself
So doggone far ahead,
Because your mouth's big enough
And that's bleached wool on your head.

Going to town with that shape,
Going to town;
Going to town with that mouth,
Going to town;
Going to town with those eyes,
Going to town.

But if you got wise to it, yellow girl,
If you only knew:
I'm sticking to my black girl
And I don't need nothing from you.

NEGRO BEMBON

¿Po qué te pone tan brabo
cuando te disen negro bembón,
si tiene la boca santa,
negro bembón?

Bembón así como ere
tiene de to;
Caridá te mantiene,
te lo da to.

Te queja todabía,
negro bembón;
sin pega y con harina,
negro bembón;
majagua de dril blanco,
negro bembón;
sapato de do tono,
negro bembón.

Bembón así como ere
tiene de to;
Caridá te mantiene,
te lo da to.

Sóngoro cosongo

BIG-LIPPED NEGRO

Why get a chip on your shoulder
When they call you big-lipped Negro,
If that mouth is good for loving,
Big-lipped Negro?

Big as your lips are,
You got plenty,
Charity's keeping you,
You got it easy!

What are you kicking for,
Big-lipped Negro?
Out of work but in the money,
Big-lipped Negro.
You got a white linen suit on,
Big-lipped Negro.
You got two-colored shoes on,
Big-lipped Negro.

Big as your lips are,
You got plenty,
Charity's keeping you,
You got it easy!

BALADA DE LOS DOS ABUELOS

A Felito Ayón

Sombras que sólo yo veo,
me escoltan mis dos abuelos.

Lanza con punta de hueso,
tambor de cuero y madera:
mi abuelo negro.

Gorguera en el cuello ancho,
gris armadura guerrera:
mi abuelo blanco.

Pie desnudo, torso pétreo
los de mi negro;
pupilas de vidrio antártico,
las de mi blanco!

Africa de selvas húmedas
y de gordos gongos sordos . . .
—Me muero!
(Dice mi abuelo negro).
Aguaprieta de caimanes,
verdes mañanas de cocos.
—Me canso!
(Dice mi abuelo blanco).
Oh velas de amargo viento,
galeón ardiendo en oro.
—Me muero!
(Dice mi abuelo negro).
Oh costas de cuello virgen,
engañadas de abalorios.
—Me canso!

BALLAD OF THE TWO GRANDFATHERS

To Felito Ayón

Shadows I alone can see,
My two grandfathers guard me.

Lance with head of bone,
Drum of wood and leather:
My black grandfather.

Ruff, wide at the throat,
Gray warrior's armor:
My white grandfather.

Naked feet, rocky torso,
These from my black man;
Pupils of antarctic glass,
These from my white man!

Africa with steaming forest
And with heavy muffled gongs . . .
—I am dying!
(Says my black grandfather.)
Dark rivers of crocodiles,
Green mornings of coco palms.
—I am weary!
(Says my white grandfather.)
O sails with bitter winds,
Galleon burning golden.
—I am dying!
(Says my black grandfather.)
O coasts with virgin throats,
Cheated with glass trinkets.
I am weary!

(Dice mi abuelo blanco).
Oh puro sol repujado,
preso en el aro del Trópico;
oh luna redonda y limpia
sobre el sueño de los monos . . .

¡Qué de barcos, qué de barcos!
¡Qué de negros, qué de negros!
¡Qué largo fulgor de cañas!
¡Qué látigo el del negrero!
¿Sangre? Sangre. ¿Llanto? Llanto . . .
Venas y ojos entreabiertos,
y madrugadas vacías,
y atardeceres de ingenio,
y una gran voz, fuerte voz,
despedazando el silencio.
¡Qué de barcos, qué de barcos!
¡Qué de negros!

Sombras que sólo yo veo,
me escoltan mis dos abuelos.

Don Federico me grita,
y Taita Facundo calla;
los dos en la noche sueñan,
y andan, andan.
Yo los junto.

     —Federico!
Facundo! Los dos se abrazan.
Los dos suspiran. Los dos
las fuertes cabezas alzan,
los dos del mismo tamaño
bajo las estrellas altas;
los dos del mismo tamaño,
ansia negra y ansia blanca,
los dos del mismo tamaño,

(Says my white grandfather.)
O clear, hammered sun,
Caught in the hoop of the tropics,
O moon limpid and full
Above the sleep of the monkeys . . .

How many ships, how many ships!
How many Negroes, how many Negroes!
What broad brilliance of sugar canes!
What lashes of the slave trader!
Blood? Blood. Tears? Tears . . .
Half-opened veins and eyelids
And empty daybreaks
And sunsets at the mill
And a great voice, a strong voice,
Shattering the silence.
How many ships, how many ships!
How many Negroes!

Shadows I alone can see,
My two grandfathers guard me.

Don Federico cries out to me
And Taita Facundo is silent;
And both dream on through the night,
Walking, walking.
And I bring them together.

                            —Federico!
Facundo! The two embrace each other.
Together they sigh. Together
They raise their proud heads
Beneath the stars high above them,
Both of the same stature;
Black desire and white desire,
Both of the same stature,

gritan. Sueñan. Lloran. Cantan . . .
Cantan . . . Cantan . . . Cantan!

West Indies Ltd. (1934)

SENSEMAYA

(Canto para matar una culebra)

A Gilberto Ante

Mayombe—bombe—mayombé!
Mayombe—bombe—mayombé!
Mayombe—bombe—mayombé!

La culebra tiene los ojos de vidrio;
la culebra viene, y se enreda en un palo;
con sus ojos de vidrio, en un palo,
con sus ojos de vidrio.
La culebra camina sin patas;
la culebra se esconde en la yerba;
caminando se esconde en la yerba,
caminando sin patas!

Mayombe—bombe—mayombé!
Mayombe—bombe—mayombé!
Mayombe—bombe—mayombé!

Tú le das con el hacha, y se muere:
dale ya!
No le des con el pie, que te muerde,
no le des con el pie, que se va!

Sensemayá, la culebra,
sensemayá.
Sensemayá, con sus ojos,
sensemayá.
Sensemayá, con su lengua,

Cry out. And dream. And weep. And sing . . .
And sing . . . And sing . . . And sing . . .

SENSEMAYA

(Chant for killing a snake.)

To Gilberto Ante

Mayombe—bombe—mayombé!
Mayombe—bombe—mayombé!
Mayombe—bombe—mayombé!

The snake's got eyes made of glass;
The snake he comes and wraps around a stick;
With his eyes made of glass, he wraps around a stick,
With his eyes made of glass.
The snake he travels without feet;
The snake he hides in the grass,
He travels and he hides in the grass,
Walking without feet.

Mayombe—bombe—mayombé!
Mayombe—bombe—mayombé!
Mayombe—bombe—mayombé!

Let him have it with the hatchet and he's dead:
Let him have it!
Don't do it with your foot or he'll bite you,
Don't do it with your foot or he'll get clean away!

Sensemayá, see that snake now,
Sensemayá.
Sensemayá, with those eyes of his,
Sensemayá.
Sensemayá, with that tongue of his,

sensemayá.
Sensemayá, con su boca,
sensemayá.

La culebra muerta no puede comer;
la culebra muerta no puede silbar:
no puede caminar,
no puede correr!
La culebra muerta no puede mirar;
la culebra muerta no puede beber:
no puede respirar,
no puede morder!

Mayombe—bombe—mayombé!
SENSEMAYA, LA CULEBRA
Mayombe—bombe—mayombé!
SENSEMAYÁ, NO SE MUEVE;
Mayombe—bombe—mayombé!
SENSEMÁYÁ, LA CULEBRA
Mayombe—bombe—mayombé!
SENSEMAYA, SE MURIÓ . . . !

West Indies Ltd.

BALADA DEL GÜIJE

Para Eusebia Cosme

¡Ñeque, que se vaya el ñeque!
¡Güije, que se vaya el güije!

Las turbias aguas del río
son hondas, y tienen muertos;
carapachos de tortuga,
cabezas de niños negros.
De noche, saca sus brazos
el río, y rasga el silencio

Sensemayá.
Sensemayá, with that mouth of his,
Sensemayá!

That snake when he's dead can't eat any more;
That snake when he's dead can't hiss any more:
Can't travel any more,
Can't run any more!
That snake when he's dead can't look any more;
That snake when he's dead can't drink any more:
Can't breathe any more,
Can't bite any more!

Mayombe—bombe—mayombé!
SENSEMAYÁ, SEE THAT SNAKE NOW
Mayombe—bombe—mayombé!
SENSEMAYÁ, HE LIES QUIET
Mayombe—bombe—mayombé!
SENSEMAYÁ, SEE THAT SNAKE NOW
Mayombe—bombe—mayombé!
SENSEMAYÁ, HE'S DEAD . . . !

BALLAD OF THE GÜIJE *

For Eusebia Cosme

Witchery, watch out for witchery!
The Güije, watch out for the Güije!

The turbid waters of the river
Are deep, they are full of dead men;
And the curving shells of turtles
And the heads of Negro babies.
At night he draws his arms out,
That river, and rips at the silence

* The Güije is a malignant Afro-Cuban water spirit.

con sus uñas, que son uñas
de cocodrilo frenético.
Bajo el grito de los astros,
bajo una luna de incendio,
ladra el río entre las piedras,
y, con invisibles dedos,
sacude el arco del puente
y estrangula a los viajeros . . .

¡Ñeque, que se vaya el ñeque!
¡Güije, que se vaya el güije!

Enanos de ombligo enorme
pueblan las aguas inquietas:
sus cortas piernas, torcidas,
sus largas orejas, rectas.
¡Ah, qué se comen mi niño
de carnes puras y negras,
y que le beben la sangre,
y que le chupan las venas,
y que le cierran los ojos,
los grandes ojos de perlas!
—¡Huye, que el coco te mata!
¡Huye, antes que el coco venga!
Mi chiquitín chiquitón,
que tu collar te proteja . . . !

¡Ñeque, que se vaya el ñeque!
¡Güije, que se vaya el güije!

Pero Changó no lo quiso . . .
Salió del agua una mano
para arrastrarlo . . . Era un güije.
Le abrió en dos tapas el cráneo,
le apagó los grandes ojos,
le arrancó los dientes blancos,
e hizo un nudo con las piernas

With his talons, sharp as the talons
Of a crocodile in a frenzy.
Under the screaming starlight,
Under the flaming moonlight,
The river creeps through the boulders
And with his invisible fingers
He shakes the arch of the bridges
And strangles the travelers . . .

Witchery, watch out for witchery!
The Güije, watch out for the Güije!

Little dwarfs with enormous navels
People the troubled waters:
Their squatty legs are twisted,
Their great big ears stand upright.
What if they should eat my baby,
The pure dark flesh of my baby,
And drink all his blood up
And suck his veins dry,
And lock up his eyelids,
Lock up his big eyes like pearls!
Run, or the Coco† will kill you!
Run, before he can get here!
My little one, O my little one,
May the necklace you wear protect you . . . !

Witchery, watch out for witchery!
The Güije, watch out for the Güije!

But Changó,‡ he wouldn't have it so . . .
A hand came out of the water
To snatch him . . . It was a Güije.
He broke his skull in two pieces,
His two big eyes were extinguished
And all his white teeth pulled out
And a knot was tied of his legs

† The Coco is a bogy used to frighten children.
‡ An African god.

y otro nudo con los brazos . . .
Mi chiquitín chiquitón,
sonrisa de gordos labios,
con el fondo de tu río
está mi pena soñando,
y con tus venitas secas,
y tu corazón mojado . . .

¡Ñeque, que se vaya el ñeque!
¡Güije, que se vaya el güije!
¡Ah, chiquitín chiquitón,
pasó lo que yo te dije!

West Indies Ltd.

D I A N A

A José Mancisidor

La diana, de madrugada,
va, con alfileres rojos,
hincando todos los ojos.
La diana, de madrugada.

Levanta en peso el cuartel
con los soldados cansados.
Van saliendo los soldados.
Levanta en peso el cuartel.

Ay diana, ya tocarás
de madrugada, algún día,
tu toque de rebeldía.
Ay diana, ya tocarás.

Vendrás a la cama dura
donde se pudre el mendigo.
—¡Amigo!—gritarás—¡Amigo!
Vendrás a la cama dura.

And another knot of his arms . . .
My little one, O my little one,
Your fat little lips are smiling,
And in the depths of your river
In my trouble I'm dreaming
Of your dry little veins
And of your wet heart . . .

Witchery, watch out for witchery!
The Güije, watch out for the Güije!
Ah, my little one, my little one,
Now heed what I say to you!

REVEILLE AT DAYBREAK

To José Mancisidor

The reveille at daybreak
Comes pricking all men's eyes
With its red brooches.
The reveille at daybreak.

It wakes the entire barracks
With the weary soldiers.
The soldiers go running forth.
It wakes the entire barracks.

Ah, reveille, you shall ring out
At daybreak, someday,
Your tocsin of rebellion.
Ah, reveille, you shall ring out.

You shall come to hard couches
Where rotting beggars lie.
And—Friend! Friend!—you shall cry.
You shall come to hard couches.

Rugirás con voz ya libre
sobre la cama de seda:
—En pie, porque nada os queda.
Rugirás con voz ya libre.

¡Fiera, fuerte, desatada,
diana en corneta de fuego,
diana del pobre y del ciego,
diana de la madrugada!

*Cantos para soldados y sones
para turistas* (1937)

You shall roar with a voice of freedom
Over the silken bedstead,
—Arise, for nothing is left you!—
You shall roar with a voice of freedom.

Proud, strong, untrammeled,
Reveille with trumpet of fire,
Reveille of the poor and the blind,
Reveille at daybreak!

PABLO NERUDA
(Neftalí Ricardo Reyes Basualto)

b. 1904, Parral, Chile

PABLO NERUDA
Neftalí Ricardo Reyes Basualto
b. 1904, Parral, Chile

NERUDA is generally considered the most important contemporary Latin American poet. He was educated in Santiago de Chile and early in life entered upon a diplomatic career. He has held positions as consul in Madrid, Calcutta, and Rangoon. At present he is consul general for Chile in Mexico. Neruda's early work shows many influences. He has passed through a more or less postmodernist phase, has learned something from Walt Whitman, and studied Blake (whom he translated) and Lautréamont. The famous Neruda style of the later books has been called surrealist but Neruda's originality transcends the ordinary surrealist methods. His poetry does not drift along on a stream of fortuitous association; he is rather trying to say many things at once about very definite emotions. He creates a counterpoint of moods and images, juxtaposing the traditionally poetic with the intentionally unpoetic, a device which gives his style its particular texture. Neruda's later work is a hallucinated vision of tragedy and corruption. He weaves a fairly precise set of personal symbols in and out of distorted fragments of reality. If the surrealists write dream poetry, it is accurate to say that Neruda dreams with his eyes open. He is the prophet of decay and his grim panoramas and exacerbated eroticism sometimes approach epic stature—his poems are fragments of a modern Inferno. In his last book, which deals with the Spanish War, he states a belief, and this brings about a change in his style. The tempo of the verse is faster, the personal symbols tend to disappear, and the poetry as a whole is more realistic in tone. If his work continues in this direction, it will mean he has entered a new phase, and *Residencia en la tierra III*, of which these hymns to Spain are to be a part, will, when it is finally published, mark a new chapter in his development. The strength of his influence today is attested by the number of his imitators all over Spanish America.

"Barrio sin luz" is here included because it is a simple statement of a mood which reappears very often in the later poems. No. XVII of "Veinte poemas" has been chosen as a sample of an intermediate phase in which traces of the mature Neruda style begin to appear. "Alberto Rojas Jiménez, viene volando," written on the occasion of the death of a young Chilean poet and critic in 1931, is one of Neruda's best-known poems and also one of his finest achievements. Against realistic funeral details, the poet creates a dreamlike flying figure of his friend and then extends the symbol until it includes an entire landscape of the imagination and expresses the writer's attitude of revulsion toward all existence. The poem is at once an elegy and a criticism of modern life. According to Amado Alonso, water, swallows, and fish are death symbols while notaries suggest the destructiveness of the commonplace. Similarly, poppies, bees, sugar, and rose bushes are symbols of affirmation and fruitfulness. While such interpretations are only approximate, it can be seen that Neruda does weave these symbols into the poem like a kind of cipher. The "Oda solar" is the last section of a series of hymns to the Spanish people which form one long poem.

La canción de la fiesta. Santiago de Chile, 1921.
Crepusculario. Santiago de Chile, 1923.
Veinte poemas de amor y una canción desesperada. Santiago de Chile, 1924.
Tentativa del hombre infinito. Santiago de Chile, 1928.
Residencia en la tierra I. Santiago de Chile, 1933.
El hondero entusiasta. Santiago de Chile, 1933.
Residencia en la tierra II. Santiago de Chile, 1935.
España en el corazón. Santiago de Chile, 1937.
Las furias y las penas. Buenos Aires, 1939.

BARRIO   SIN   LUZ

¿Se va la poesía de las cosas
o no la puede condensar mi vida?
Ayer—mirando el último crepúsculo—
yo era un manchón de musgo entre unas ruinas.

Las ciudades—hollines y venganzas—
la cochinada gris de los suburbios,
la oficina que encorva las espaldas,
el jefe de ojos turbios.

. . . Sangre de un arrebol sobre los cerros,
sangre sobre las calles y las plazas,
dolor de corazones rotos,
podre de hastíos y de lágrimas.

Un río abraza el arrabal como una
mano helada que tienta en las tinieblas;
sobre sus aguas
se avergüenzan de verse las estrellas.

Y las casas que esconden los deseos
detrás de las ventanas luminosas,
mientras afuera el viento
lleva un poco de barro a cada rosa.

. . . Lejos . . . la bruma de las olvidanzas,
—humos espesos, tajamares rotos—
y el campo ¡el campo verde! en que jadean
los bueyes y los hombres sudorosos.

. . . Y aquí estoy yo, brotado entre las ruinas,
mordiendo sólo todas las tristezas,
como si el llanto fuera una semilla
y yo el único surco de la tierra.

Crepusculario (1923)

LIGHTLESS SUBURB

Must the poetry of everything vanish
Or can my life ever condense it?
Yesterday—watching the last twilight—
I was a patch of moss among ruins.

Cities—black and revengeful—
The swinish gray of the suburbs,
The office that bends our shoulders,
The boss with muddy eyes.

. . . Blood of a cloudy sky over the hills,
Blood on the streets and the squares,
Sorrow of tattered hearts,
Pus of disgust and weeping.

A river embraces the outskirts
Like an icy hand that gropes in the shadows;
In its waters
The stars are ashamed to see themselves.

And the houses that hide desires
Behind the luminous windows,
While outside the wind is carrying
A little clay to each rose.

. . . Far off . . . the mist of forgetfulness—
Murky vapors, ragged bridge piers—
And the country, the green country! where oxen
And sweaty men are panting.

. . . And here am I, budding among the ruins
With only sorrow to bite on,
As if weeping were a seed and I
The earth's only furrow.

NO. XVII

Pensando, enredando sombras en la profunda soledad.
Tú también estás lejos, ah más lejos que nadie,
Pensando, soltando pájaros, desvaneciendo imágenes,
enterrando lámparas.

Campanario de brumas, qué lejos, allá arriba!
Ahogando lamentos, moliendo esperanzas sombrías,
molinero taciturno,
se te viene de bruces la noche, lejos de la ciudad.

Tu presencia es ajena, extraña a mí como una cosa.
Pienso, camino largamente, mi vida antes de ti.
Mi vida antes de nadie, mi áspera vida.
El grito frente al mar, entre las piedras,
corriendo libre, loco, en el vaho del mar.
La furia triste, el grito, la soledad del mar.
Desbocado, violento, estirado hacia el cielo.

Tú, mujer, qué eras allí, qué raya, qué varilla
de ese abanico inmenso? Estabas lejos como ahora.
Incendio en el bosque! Arde en cruces azules.
Arde, arde, llamea, chispea en árboles de luz.
Se derrumba, crepita. Incendio. Incendio.
Y mi alma baila herida de virutas de fuego.
Quién llama? Que silencio poblado de ecos?
Hora de la nostalgia, hora de la alegría, hora de soledad,
Hora mía, entre todas!

Bocina en que el viento pasa cantando.
Tanta pasión de llanto anudada a mi cuerpo.
Sacudida de todas las raíces,
Asalto de todas las olas!
Rodaba, alegre, triste, interminable, mi alma.

Pensando, enterrando lámparas en la profunda soledad.
Quién eres tú, quién eres?

*Veinte poemas de amor y una canción
desesperada* (1924)

N O . X V I I

Thinking, entangling shadows in deep solitude.
You, too, are far away, alas much farther than anyone,
Thinking, setting birds free, dimming images,
Burying lamps.

Belfry of mist, how far up yonder!
Choking lamentations, grinding dark hopes,
Taciturn miller,
Night falls headlong in front of you, far from the city.

Your presence is alien, strange to me like an object.
I think, I walk for a long time, my life before you.
My life before anyone, my acrid life.
The yell facing the sea, among the stones,
Flowing freely, madly, in the sea vapor.
Sad fury, the yell, the solitude of the sea.
Unbridled, violent, stretched toward the sky.

You, woman, what were you there, what stripe, what rib
Of this immense fan? You were as far away as now.
Fire in the woods! It burns in blue crosses.
It burns, it burns, it flames, it sparkles in trees of light.
It crumples, it crackles. Fire. Fire.
And my soul dances, wounded by splinters of fire.
Who calls? What silence, peopled by echoes?
Hour of nostalgia, hour of joy, hour of solitude,
Hour of mine, among all others!

Trumpet through which the wind passes singing.
So much passion of weeping knotted in my body.
All roots shaken off,
Assault of all the waves!
My soul wandered, joyful, sad, interminable.

Thinking, burying lamps in profound solitude.
Who are you then, who are you?

SABOR

De falsas astrologías de costumbres un tanto lúgubres,
vertidas en lo inacabable, y siempre llevadas al lado,
he conservado una tendencia, un sabor solitario,

De conversaciones gastadas como usadas maderas,
con humildad de sillas, con palabras ocupadas
en servir como esclavos de voluntad secundaria,
teniendo esa consistencia de la leche, de las semanas muertas,
del aire encadenado sobre las ciudades.

Quién puede jactarse de paciencia más sólida?
La cordura me envuelve de piel compacta
de un color reunido como una culebra:
mis criaturas nacen de un largo rechazo:
ay, con un solo alcohol puedo despedir este día
que he elegido, igual entre los días terrestres.

Vivo lleno de una substancia de color común silenciosa
como una vieja madre, una paciencia fija
como sombra de iglesia o reposo de huesos.

Voy lleno de esas aguas dispuestas profundamente,
preparadas, durmiéndose en una atención triste.

En mi interior de guitarra hay un aire viejo,
seco y sonoro, permanecido, inmóvil,
como una nutrición fiel, como humo:
un elemento en descanso, un aceite vivo:
un pájaro de rigor cuida mi cabeza:
un ángel invariable vive en mi espada.

Residencia en la tierra I (1933)

SAVOR

From false astrologies with somewhat lugubrious manners,
Poured into the ineffable and always kept close at hand,
I have preserved an inclination, a solitary savor,

From wasted conversations like secondhand boards,
From the humility of chairs, from words
Occupied with service, like weak-willed slaves,
Possessing the consistency of milk, from dead weeks,
From the air enchained above cities.

Who can boast of a more solid patience?
Sanity enfolds me with a compact skin
Coiled like the color of a snake:
My children are born of a long rejection:
Ah, with a single alcohol I can dismiss this day
I have just elected, the same among all terrestrial days.

I live full of a substance with an ordinary color,
Silent as an old mother, a fixed patience,
Like the shadow of a church, like the repose of bones.

I am full of those waters deeply composed,
In readiness, sleeping with sad attentiveness.

In my guitar interior I have an old air,
Dry and sonorous, permanent, motionless,
Like a faithful nutriment, like smoke:
An element in repose, a live oil:
A bird of severity guards my head:
An unvarying angel lives in my sword.

ODA CON UN LAMENTO

Oh niña entre las rosas, oh presión de palomas,
oh presidio de peces y rosales,
tu alma es una botella llena de sal sedienta
y una campana llena de uvas es tu piel.

Por desgracia no tengo para darte sino uñas
o pestañas, o pianos derretidos,
o sueños que salen de mi corazón a borbotones,
polvorientos sueños que corren como jinetes negros,
sueños llenos de velocidades y desgracias.

Sólo puedo quererte con besos y amapolas,
con guirnaldas mojadas por la lluvia,
mirando cenicientos caballos y perros amarillos.

Sólo puedo quererte con olas a la espalda,
entre vagos golpes de azufre y aguas ensimismadas,
nadando en contra de los cementerios que corren
    en ciertos ríos
con pasto mojado creciendo sobre las tristes tumbas
    de yeso,
nadando a través de corazones sumergidos
y pálidas planillas de niños insepultos.
Hay mucha muerte, muchos acontecimientos funerarios
en mis desamparadas pasiones y desolados besos,
hay el agua que cae en mi cabeza,
mientras crece mi pelo,
un agua como el tiempo, un agua negra desencadenada,
con una voz nocturna, con un grito
de pájaro en la lluvia, como una interminable
sombra de ala mojada que protege mis huesos,
mientras me visto, mientras
interminablemente me miro en los espejos y en los
    vidrios,

ODE WITH A LAMENT

O girl among the roses, O pressure of doves,
O citadel of fishes and rosebushes,
Your soul is a bottle full of dry salt
And your skin is a bell full of grapes.

Unfortunately I have nothing to give you except fingernails
Or eyelashes, or melted pianos,
Or dreams which pour from my heart in torrents,
Dusty dreams that race like black riders,
Dreams full of speed and affliction.

I can only love you with kisses and poppies,
With garlands wet by the rain,
Gazing at yellow dogs and horses red as ashes.

I can only love you with waves behind me,
Between wandering gusts of sulphur and pensive waters,
Swimming toward cemeteries that flow in certain
        rivers
With wet pasturage growing above sad tombs of
        plaster,
Swimming through submerged hearts
And pale catalogues of unburied children.
There is much death, many funereal events
In my forsaken passions and desolate kisses,
There is a water that falls on my head,
While my hair grows,
A water like time, a black torrential water,
With a nocturnal voice, with a cry
Of a bird in the rain, like an interminable
Shadow of a wet wing sheltering my bones,
While I dress myself, while
Interminably I look at myself in mirrors and windows,

oigo que alguien me sigue llamándome a sollozos
con una triste voz podrida por el tiempo.

Tú estás de pie sobre la tierra, llena
de dientes y relámpagos.
Tú propagas los besos y matas las hormigas.
Tú lloras de salud, de cebolla, de abeja,
de abecedario ardiendo.
Tú eres como una espada azul y verde
y ondulas al tocarte, como un río.

Ven a mi alma vestida de blanco, como un ramo
de ensangrentadas rosas y copas de cenizas,
ven con una manzana y un caballo,
porque allí hay una sala oscura y un candelabro roto,
unas sillas torcidas que esperan el invierno,
y una paloma muerta, con un número.

Residencia en la tierra II (1935)

AGUA SEXUAL

Rodando a goterones solos,
a gotas como dientes,
a espesos goterones de mermelada y sangre,
rodando a goterones,
cae el agua,
como una espada en gotas,
como un desgarrador río de vidrio,
cae mordiendo,
golpeando el eje de la simetría, pegando en las
costuras del alma,
rompiendo cosas abandonadas, empapando lo oscuro.

Solamente es un soplo, más húmedo que el llanto,
un líquido, un sudor, un aceite sin nombre,
un movimiento agudo,
haciéndose, espesándose,

I hear someone calling me, calling me with sobs,
With a sad voice rotted by time.

You are on foot, on the earth, full
Of fangs and lightings.
You generate kisses and you kill ants.
You weep with health, with onions, with bees,
With burning alphabet.
You are like a blue and green sword
And you ripple when touched like a river.

Come to my soul dressed in white, like a branch
Of bleeding roses and cups of ashes,
Come with an apple and a horse,
Because there is a dark room there and a broken candelabra,
Some twisted chairs that wait for winter,
And a dead dove with a number.

SEXUAL WATER

Running in single drops,
In drops like teeth,
In thick drops of marmalade and blood,
Running in drops,
The water falls,
Like a sword of drops
Like a rending river of glass,
It falls biting,
Striking the axis of symmetry, hitting on the
Ribs of the soul,
Breaking castoff things, soaking the darkness.

It is only a gust, damper than tears,
A liquid, a sweat, a nameless oil,
A sharp movement,
Creating itself, thickening itself,

cae el agua,
a goterones lentos,
hacia su mar, hacia su seco océano,
hacia su ola sin agua.

Veo el verano extenso, y un estertor saliendo de
    un granero,
bodegas, cigarras,
poblaciones, estímulos,
habitaciones, niñas
durmiendo con las manos en el corazón,
soñando con bandidos, con incendios,
veo barcos,
veo árboles de médula,
erizados como gatos rabiosos,
veo sangre, puñales y medias de mujer,
y pelos de hombre,
veo camas, veo corredores donde grita una virgen,
veo frazadas y órganos y hoteles.

Veo los sueños sigilosos,
admito los postreros días,
y también los orígenes, y también los recuerdos,
como un párpado atrozmente levantado a la
    fuerza
estoy mirando.

Y entonces hay este sonido:
un ruido rojo de huesos,
un pegarse de carne,
y piernas amarillas como espigas juntándose.
Yo escucho entre el disparo de los besos,
escucho, sacudido entre respiraciones y sollozos.

Estoy mirando, oyendo,
con la mitad del alma en el mar y la mitad del
    alma en la tierra,
y con las dos mitades del alma miro el mundo.

The water falls,
In slow drops,
Toward the sea, toward its dry ocean,
Toward its wave without water.

I see a long summer and a death rattle coming out
    of a granary,
Cellars, cicadas,
Towns, stimuli,
Habitations, girl children
Sleeping with hands on their hearts,
Dreaming with pirates, with fire,
I see ships,
I see trees of spinal cord
Bristling like furious cats,
I see blood, daggers, and women's stockings,
I see men's hair,
I see beds, I see corridors where a virgin screams,
I see blankets and organs and hotels.

I see stealthy dreams,
I accept the preceding days,
And also origins and also memories,
Like an eyelid dreadfully raised by force
I am watching.

And then there is this sound:
A red noise of bones,
An adhering of flesh,
And legs yellow as grain stalks joining together.
I am listening among explosions of kisses,
I am listening, shaken among breathing and sobs.

I am watching, hearing
With half my soul on sea and half my soul
    on land,
And with both halves of my soul I look at the world.

Y aunque cierre los ojos y me cubra el corazón,
enteramente,
veo caer un agua sorda,
a goterones sordos.

Es como un huracán de gelatina,
como una catarata de espermas y medusas.
Veo correr un arco iris turbio.
Veo pasar sus aguas a través de los huesos.

Residencia en la tierra II

ALBERTO ROJAS JIMENEZ VIENE VOLANDO

Entre plumas que asustan, entre noches,
entre magnolias, entre telegramas,
entre el viento del Sur y el Oeste marino,
        vienes volando.

Bajo las tumbas, bajo las cenizas,
bajo los caracoles congelados,
bajo las últimas aguas terrestres,
        vienes volando.

Más abajo, entre niñas sumergidas,
y plantas ciegas, y pescados rotos,
más abajo, entre nubes otra vez,
        vienes volando.

Más allá de la sangre y de los huesos,
más allá del pan, más allá del vino,
más allá del fuego,
        vienes volando.

Más allá del vinagre y de la muerte,
entre putrefacciones y violetas,

And though I close my eyes and cover my heart
Completely,
I see a deaf water falling
In deaf drops.

It is like a hurricane of gelatin,
Like a cataract of sperm and medusas.
I see a muddy rainbow flowing.
I see its waters passing through my bones.

ALBERTO ROJAS JIMENEZ
COMES FLYING

Between fearful feathers, between the nights,
Between the magnolias, between telegrams,
Between the south wind and the sea wind of the west,
        You come flying.

Below tombs, below ashes,
Below frozen snails,
Below the deepest terrestrial waters,
        You come flying.

Lower still, among submerged girl-children
And blind plants and wounded fishes,
Lower still, once more among clouds,
        You come flying.

Farther than the blood, farther than the bones,
Farther than bread, farther than wine,
Farther than fire,
        You come flying.

Farther than vinegar and death,
Among putrefactions and violets,

con tu celeste voz y tus zapatos húmedos,
vienes volando.

Sobre diputaciones y farmacias,
y ruedas, y abogados, y navíos,
y dientes rojos recién arrancados,
vienes volando.

Sobre ciudades de tejado hundido
en que grandes mujeres se destrenzan
con anchas manos y peines perdidos,
vienes volando.

Junto a bodegas donde el vino crece
con tibias manos turbias, en silencio,
con lentas manos de madera roja,
vienes volando.

Entre aviadores desaparecidos,
al lado de canales y de sombras,
al lado de azucenas enterradas,
vienes volando.

Entre botellas de color amargo,
entre anillos de anís y desventura,
levantando las manos y llorando,
vienes volando.

Sobre dentistas y congregaciones,
sobre cines, y túneles, y orejas,
con traje nuevo y ojos extinguidos,
vienes volando.

Sobre tu cementerio sin paredes
donde los marineros se extravían,
mientras la lluvia de tu muerte cae,
vienes volando.

With your celestial voice and your moist shoes,
          You come flying.

Above deputations and drugstores
And wheels and lawyers and ocean liners
And red teeth, recently extracted,
          You come flying.

Above cities with submerged roof tops,
In which large women unplait their hair
With broad hands and lost combs,
          You come flying.

Close to a cellar where the wine matures,
With tepid, muddy hands, in silence,
With slow hands, red and wooden,
          You come flying.

Among vanished aviators,
Beside canals and shadows,
Beside buried white lilies,
          You come flying.

Among bottles with a bitter color,
Among rings of anise seed and misfortune,
Raising your hands and weeping,
          You come flying.

Over dentists and congregations,
Over cinemas, ears, and tunnels,
In a new suit, with extinguished eyes,
          You come flying.

Over your unwalled cemetery
Where the sailors go astray,
While the rain of your death falls,
          You come flying.

Mientras la lluvia de tus dedos cae,
mientras la lluvia de tus huesos cae,
mientras tu médula y tu risa caen,
　　　vienes volando.

Sobre las piedras en que te derrites,
corriendo, invierno abajo, tiempo abajo,
mientras tu corazón desciende en gotas,
　　　vienes volando.

No estás allí, rodeado de cemento,
y negros corazones de notarios,
y enfurecidos huesos de jinetes:
　　　vienes volando.

Oh amapola marina, oh deudo mío,
oh guitarrero vestido de abejas,
no es verdad tanta sombra en tus cabellos:
　　　vienes volando.

No es verdad tanta sombra persiguiéndote,
no es verdad tantas golondrinas muertas,
tanta región oscura con lamentos:
　　　vienes volando.

El viento negro de Valparaíso
abre sus alas de carbón y espuma
para barrer el cielo donde pasas:
　　　vienes volando.

Hay vapores, y un frío de mar muerto,
y silbatos, y meses, y un olor
de mañana lloviendo y peces sucios:
　　　vienes volando.

Hay ron, tú y yo, y mi alma donde lloro,
y nadie y nada, sino una escalera

While the rain of your fingers falls,
While the rain of your bones falls,
While your marrow and your laughter fall,
     You come flying.

Over the stones into which you are melting,
Flowing, down winter, down time,
While your heart descends in a shower of drops,
     You come flying.

You are not there, circled with cement
And the black hearts of notaries
And the maddened bones of riders:
     You come flying.

O poppy of the sea, O my kinsman,
O guitar player dressed in bees,
It is not true there is all this shadow in your hair:
     You come flying.

It is not true that all this shadow pursues you,
It is not true there are all these dead swallows,
All this obscure region of lamentation:
     You come flying.

The black wind of Valparaiso
Spreads its wings of smoke and foam
To sweep the sky where you pass:
     You come flying.

There are steamers and the cold of a dead sea
And whistles and months and an odor
Of a rainy morning and filthy fishes:
     You come flying.

There is rum, and you and I, and my soul that I weep in,
And no one and nothing, except for a staircase

de peldaños quebrados, y un paraguas:
vienes volando.

Allí está el mar. Bajo de noche y te oigo
venir volando bajo el mar sin nadie,
bajo el mar que me habita, oscurecido:
vienes volando.

Oigo tus alas y tu lento vuelo,
y el agua de los muertos me golpea
como palomas ciegas y mojadas:
vienes volando.

Vienes volando, solo, solitario,
solo entre muertos, para siempre solo,
vienes volando sin sombra y sin nombre,
sin azúcar, sin boca, sin rosales,
vienes volando.

Residencia en la tierra II

O D A   S O L A R   A L   E J E R C I T O
D E L   P U E B L O

Armas del pueblo! Aquí! La amenaza, el asedio
aun derraman la tierra mezclándola de muerte,
áspera de aguijones! Salud, salud,
salud te dicen las madres del mundo,
las escuelas te dicen salud, los viejos carpinteros,
Ejército del Pueblo, te dicen salud, con las espigas,
la leche, las patatas, el limón, el laurel,
todo lo que es de la tierra y de la boca
del hombre.
Todo, como un collar
de manos, como una
cintura palpitante, como una obstinación de relámpagos,
todo a ti se prepara, todo hacia ti converge!
Día de hierro,

With broken steps and an umbrella:
> You come flying.

There is the sea. I descend at night and I hear you
Come flying below the deserted sea,
Below the sea that lives in me, in obscurity:
> You come flying.

I hear your wings and your slow flight
And the water of the dead strikes me
Like blind moist doves:
> You come flying.

You come flying, alone, solitary,
Alone among corpses, forever alone,
You come flying without a shadow, nameless,
Without sugar, without a mouth, without rosebushes,
> You come flying.

ODE OF THE SUN TO THE PEOPLE'S ARMY

Arms of the people! This way! Menace and siege
Still are wasting the earth, mixing it with death,
With the sharpness of goads! Salud, salud,
The mothers of the world cry salud to you,
The schools cry salud, the old carpenters,
Army of the People, they cry salud with ears of grain,
With milk, with potatoes, with the lemon and the laurel,
All that is of the earth and the mouth
Of man.
> All, like a necklace
Of hands, like a
Palpitating girdle, like the obstinacy of lightning,
All prepares for you, all converges toward you!
> Day of steel,

azul fortificado!
      Hermanos, adelante,
adelante por las tierras aradas,
adelante en la noche seca y sin sueño, delirante y raída,
adelante entre vides, pisando el color frío de las rocas,
salud, salud, seguid. Más cortantes que la voz del invierno,
más sensibles que el párpado, más seguros que la punta del
      trueno,
puntuales como el rápido diamante, nuevamente marciales,
guerreros según el agua acerada de las tierras del centro,
según la flor y el vino, según el corazón espiral de la tierra,
según las raíces de todas las hojas, de todas las mercaderías
      fragantes de la tierra.
Salud, soldados, salud, barbechos rojos,
salud, tréboles duros, salud, pueblos parados
en la luz del relámpago, salud, salud, salud,
adelante, adelante, adelante, adelante,
sobre las minas, sobre los cementerios, frente al abominable
apetito de muerte, frente al erizado
terror de los traidores,
pueblo, pueblo eficaz, corazón y fusiles,
corazón y fusiles, adelante.
Fotógrafos, mineros, ferroviarios, hermanos
del carbón y la piedra, parientes del martillo,
bosque, fiesta de alegres disparos, adelante,
guerilleros, mayores, sargentos, comisarios políticos,
aviadores del pueblo, combatientes nocturnos,
combatientes marinos, adelante:
frente a vosotros
no hay más que una mortal cadena, un agujero
de podridos pescados: adelante!
no hay allí sino muertos moribundos,
pantanos de terrible pus sangrienta,
no hay enemigos: adelante, España,

Fortified blueness!
   Forward, brothers,
Forward through the plowed fields,
Forward through the dry and sleepless night, threadbare and
  delirious,
Forward among grapevines, treading the cold color of the
  rocks,
Salud, salud, press on! Sharper than the voice of winter,
More sensitive than the eyelid, more certain than the point
  of thunder,
Punctual as the swift diamond, new in warfare,
Warriors like steel gray water of the midlands,
Like the flower and the wine, like the spiral heart of the
  earth,
Like the roots of all the leaves, of all the fragrant merchan-
  dise of the earth.
Salud, soldiers, salud, red plow furrows,
Salud, sturdy clover, salud, ranks of the people
In the light of the lightning, salud, salud, salud,
Forward, forward, forward, forward,
Over the mines, over the cemeteries, against the abominable
Appetite of death, against the spiny
Terror of traitors,
People, capable people, heart and rifles,
Heart and rifles, forward.
Photographers, miners, railworkers, brothers
Of the coal mine and stone quarry, kinsmen
Of the hammer, the forest, joyful shooting festival, forward,
Guerrillas, majors, sergeants, political commissars,
Aviators of the people, night fighters,
Sea fighters, forward!
Against you
There is nothing but a human chain gang, a pit full
Of rotten fish; forward!
There is nothing but dying corpses,
Swamps of terrible bloody pus,
There are no enemies: forward, Spain,

adelante, campanas populares,
adelante, regiones de manzana,
adelante, estandartes cereales,
adelante, mayúsculas del fuego,
porque en la lucha, en la ola, en la pradera,
en la montaña, en el crepúsculo cargado de acre aroma,
lleváis un nacimiento de permanencia, un hilo
de difícil dureza.
        Mientras tanto,
raíz y guirnalda sube del silencio
para esperar la mineral victoria:
cada instrumento, cada rueda roja,
cada mango de sierra o penacho de arado,
cada extracción del suelo, cada temblor de sangre
quiere seguir tus pasos, Ejército del Pueblo:
tu luz organizada llega a los pobres hombres
olvidados, tu definida estrella
clava sus roncos rayos en la muerte
y establece los nuevos ojos de la esperanza.

España en el corazón (1937)

Forward, bells of the people,
Forward, regions of apple orchards,
Forward, banners of grain,
Forward, capital letters of fire,
For in the struggle on the waves, in the fields,
In the mountains, in the twilight loaded with acrid perfume,
You are giving birth to permanence, a thread
Of difficult strength.
          In the meanwhile,
Root and garland arise from silence
To await the ore of victory:
Each tool, each red wheel,
Each saw handle, the plume of each plow,
Each product of soil, each tremor of blood
Seeks to follow your footsteps, Army of the People:
Your organized light reaches the poor,
The forgotten men, your definite star
Nails its hoarse rays in death
And enacts the new eyes of hope.

CESAR VALLEJO

b. 1895, Santiago de Chuco, Peru. d. 1938, Paris

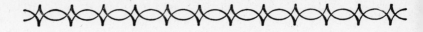

CESAR VALLEJO
b. 1895, Santiago de Chuco, Peru. d. 1938, Paris

VALLEJO is a poet whose true stature has only begun to be appreciated since his recent and untimely death. He grew up in a provincial environment, his father having been governor of his native village. This background is reflected in his first book, a pessimistic and nostalgic interpretation of small-town life, which was received with critical indifference. Its directness of statement and bareness of rhetoric constitute a break with modernism. Vallejo was educated in Trujillo and the University of Lima. He belonged to the literary group of Trujillo and later taught in the secondary schools of Lima. He paid a visit to the village of his birth when his mother died in 1920. Here, as a result of a local intrigue against him, he was subjected to judicial persecution on a trumped-up charge and held some months in jail. During this time he wrote some of the poetry which appeared in his second book, *Trilce*. His friends came to his aid and helped to clear him of all charges, but the poet no longer wished to remain in his own country. In 1923 he went to Paris, thereafter living the life of an expatriate in Paris and Madrid. He also spent some time traveling in Russia. Through his later years he barely supported himself by journalism, and when he died he was starving.

Vallejo was one of the chief initiators of the contemporary movement in Peru. Since his work is many sided, it has provoked a great variety of critical comment. Perhaps on the basis of his mixed blood, Arturo Torres Ríoseco sees him as a mystic. Núñez claims that his treatment of family life and provincial Peru links him with indigenism, and compares his vanguardist style with German expressionism. Actually, in all his work there is an almost painful sincerity, a primitive disregard of literary elegance. His mature poetry is often very difficult, not because of literary obscurantism but because of the complexity and intensity of his imagination. Multiplicity of reference and compound images create a very dense texture. As he developed, his humanity, his profound and passionate desire for social progress deepened. A sympathy for suffering, a sense of the eternal tragedy in ordinary lives, is fundamental in all his work. His poems dealing with the Spanish War are some of the most lofty and heroic that have yet been written on that theme. Much of Vallejo's work, including several plays and a group of essays, remains unpublished. Spanish and Peruvian critics agree that he is one of the great poets of our time.

"Los pasos lejanos," it should be noted, deals with a postmodernist theme but gives it a new treatment. No. XVIII from *Trilce* was written while the poet was in prison. The three poems included here from *Trilce* illustrate a progression from the provincial phase to extreme vanguardism. No. XLVI bears comparison to the poetry of Huidobro; in fact José Bergamín describes Vallejo as a creationist. "Los nueve monstruos" is an example of Vallejo's most difficult style. The marxist inspiration is never explicit, it is absorbed into the poet's infinite compassion for suffering. The style is tortured, rugged, as if the writer were struggling to find adequate symbols, as if the intensity of his vision overflowed the limitations of words. And yet the actual material of the poem is earthy and realistic. "Pedro Rojas" is one of the finest of the war poems. Vallejo has here achieved a new kind of realism, raised to a plane of nobility and heroic dignity.

Los heraldos negros. Trujillo, 1918.
Escalas melografiadas (stories). Lima, 1922.
Trilce. Lima, 1922.
Fabla salvaje (novel). Lima, 1923.
El tungsteno (play). Madrid, 1931.
Rusia 1931 (prose). Madrid, 1931.
Poemas humanos (edited by his wife). Paris, 1939.
España, aparta de mí este cáliz. Mexico City, 1940.
Antología de César Vallejo (edited by Xavier Abril). Buenos Aires, 1942.

LOS HERALDOS NEGROS

Hay golpes en la vida, tan fuertes. ¡Yo no sé!
Golpes como del odio de Dios; como si ante ellos,
la resaca de todo lo sufrido
se empozara en el alma. ¡Yo no sé!

Son pocos; pero son. Abren zanjas obscuras
en el rostro más fiero y en lomo más fuerte.
Serán tal vez los potros de bárbaros atilas;
o los heraldos negros que nos manda la Muerte.

Son las hondas caídas de los Cristos del alma,
de una fe adorable que el Destino blasfema.
Estos golpes sangrientos son las crepitaciones
de algún pan que en la puerta del horno se nos quema.

Y el hombre. Pobre. ¡Pobre! Vuelve los ojos, como
cuando por sobre el hombro nos llama una palmada;
vuelve los ojos locos, y todo lo vivido
se empoza, como charco de culpa, en la mirada.

Hay golpes en la vida, tan fuertes. ¡Yo no sé!

Los heraldos negros (1918)

THE BLACK MESSENGERS

In life there are blows so heavy. "I don't know."
Blows like God's hatred; as if before them
The undertow of all that is suffered
Should be dammed up in the soul. "I don't know."

There are few; but they exist. Dark chasms
Open in the boldest face and in the strongest back.
Perhaps they shall be the steeds of barbaric Attilas
Or the black messengers that death sends us.

They are the profound backslidings of Christs of the soul
From an adored faith, blasphemed by destiny.
These bloody blows are the cracklings
Of some bread that we have burned in the door of the oven.

And man. Wretch! Wretch! He turns his eyes,
As if behind our backs a clap of hands summons us;
He turns mad eyes and all that has been lived
Is dammed up like a puddle of blame in his look.

In life there are blows so heavy. "I don't know."

LA ARAÑA

Es una araña enorme que ya no anda;
una araña incolora, cuyo cuerpo,
una cabeza y un abdomen, sangra.

Hoy la he visto de cerca. Y con qué esfuerzo
hacia todos los flancos
sus pies innumerables alargaba.
Y he pensado en sus ojos invisibles,
los pilotos fatales de la araña.

Es una araña que temblaba fija
en un filo de piedra;
el abdomen a un lado,
y al otro la cabeza.

Con tantos pies la pobre, y aún no puede
resolverse. Y, al verla
atónita en tal trance,
hoy me ha dado qué pena esa viajera.

Es una araña enorme, a quien impide
el abdomen seguir a la cabeza.
Y he pensado en sus ojos
y en sus pies numerosos.
¡Y me ha dado qué pena esa viajera!

Los heraldos negros

THE SPIDER

It is an enormous spider that no longer moves;
A colorless spider, whose body,
A head and an abdomen, is bleeding.

Today I have seen it from close by. And with what efforts
Toward all sides
It was stretching its innumerable feet!
I thought of its invisible eyes,
The spider's fatal pilots.

It is a spider that quivered, caught
On the edge of a stone,
The abdomen on one side,
The head on the other.

Poor thing with so many feet and still it cannot
Find a solution. And, seeing it
Stupefied in such an emergency,
How I am troubled today by that traveler!

It is an enormous spider, whose abdomen
Keeps it from following its head.
And I thought of its eyes
And its numerous feet.
And how I am troubled by that traveler!

LOS PASOS LEJANOS

Mi padre duerme. Su semblante augusto
figura un apacible corazón;
está ahora tan dulce . . .
si hay algo en él de amargo, seré yo,

Hay soledad en el hogar; se reza;
y no hay noticias de los hijos hoy.
Mi padre se despierta, ausculta
la huída a Egipto, el restañante adiós.
Está ahora tan cerca;
si hay algo en él de lejos, seré yo.

Y mi madre pasea allá en los huertos,
saboreando un sabor ya sin sabor.
Está ahora tan suave,
tan ala, tan salida, tan amor.

Hay soledad en el hogar sin bulla,
sin noticias, sin verde, sin niñez.
Y si hay algo quebrado en esta tarde,
y que baja y que cruje,
son dos viejos caminos blancos, curvos.
Por ellos va mi corazón a pie.

Los heraldos negros

DISTANT FOOTSTEPS

My father sleeps. His august face
Expresses a peaceful heart.
He is so sweet now . . .
If there is anything bitter in him, it will be I.

There is solitude in the house; there is prayer;
There is no news of his sons today.
My father rouses, he listens
To the flight into Egypt, the stanching farewell.
He is so close now;
If there is anything distant in him, it will be I.

My mother walks in the orchard yonder,
Tasting a taste already tasteless.
She is so gentle now,
So much wing, so much departure, so much love.

There is solitude in the house, without a sound,
Without news, without greenness, without childhood,
And if there is anything broken this afternoon,
And if it falls or creaks,
It is two old roadways, white and curving,
And my heart goes walking down them.

X V I I I

Oh las cuatro paredes de la celda.
Ah las cuatro paredes albicantes
que sin remedio dan al mismo número.

Criaderos de nervios, mala brecha,
por sus cuatro rincones cómo arranca
las diarias aherrojadas extremidades.

Amorosa llavera de innumerables llaves,
si estuvieras aquí, si vieras hasta
qué hora son cuatro estas paredes.
Contra ellas seríamos contigo, los dos,
más dos que nunca. ¡Y ni lloraras,
di, libertadora!

Ah las paredes de la celda.
De ellas me duelen, entretanto, más
las dos largas, que tienen esta noche
algo de madres que ya muertas
llevan por bromurados declives,
a un niño de la mano cada una.

Y sólo yo me voy quedando,
con la diestra, que hace por ambas manos,
en alto, en busca de terciario brazo
que ha de pupilar, entre mi dónde y mi cuándo,
esta mayoría inválida de hombre.

Trilce (1922)

XVIII

Oh, the four walls of the cell!
Ah, the four whitening walls
Which never fail to add up to the same number!

Seedbeds of nerves, evil aperture,
How it snatches from its four corners
At the daily chained extremities!

Kind turnkey of innumerable keys,
If you were here, if you could see
Till what hour these walls remain four,
We should both be against them, we two,
More two than ever. And neither should you weep,
Speak, O liberator!

Ah, the walls of the cell!
Meanwhile I am hurt all the more
By the two long ones which, this night, possess
Something of mothers already dead,
Each leading a child by the hand
Down bromine steeps.

And I am left alone,
The right hand upraised, which serves for both,
Seeking the third arm
Which, between my where and my when,
Must look for man's powerless superiority.

XXVIII

He almorzado solo ahora, y no he tenido
madre, ni súplica, ni sírvete, ni agua,
ni padre que, en el facundo ofertorio
de los choclos, pregunte para su tardanza
de imagen, por los broches mayores del sonido.

Cómo iba yo a almorzar. Cómo me iba a servir
de tales platos distantes esas cosas,
cuando habráse quebrado el propio hogar,
cuando no asoma ni madre a los labios.
Cómo iba yo a almorzar nonada.

A la mesa de un buen amigo he almorzado
con su padre recién llegado del mundo,
con sus canas tías que hablan
en tordillo retinte de porcelana,
bisbiseando por todos viudos alvéolos;
y con cubiertos francos de alegres tiroriros,
porque estánse en su casa. Así, ¡qué gracia!
Y me han dolido los cuchillos
de esta mesa en todo el paladar.

El yantar de estas mesas así, en que se prueba
amor ajeno en vez del propio amor,
torna tierra el bocado que no brinda la
    MADRE,
hace golpe la dura deglusión; el dulce,
hiel; aceite funéreo, el café.

Cuando ya se ha quebrado el propio hogar,
y el sírvete materno no sale de la tumba,
la cocina a obscuras, la miseria de amor.

Trilce

XXVIII

I now have lunched alone, I have had
No mother or "please" or "help yourself" or water
Or father who, over the eloquent offertory
Of green corn ears, by his statue-slowness,
Asks for the greater hooks of sound.

How was I going to lunch? How was I to serve myself
With those things from such distant plates?
When your home is broken to bits,
When no "Mother" comes to your lips,
How was I to lunch on nothing at all?

I have lunched at the table of a good friend
With his father recently returned from far away,
With his gray-haired aunts talking
In gray tinkle of china,
Whistling through all their missing teeth;
And with the gay silverware with the sound of joyful wood
    winds,
Because they were at home. And what merit in that!
And the knives of this table
Hurt me in all I tasted.

And dining at tables like these, at which you put on
An alien love instead of your own,
The mouthful not offered by your Mother turns into earth,
The difficult swallow is a blow, the desert
Gall; the coffee, funeral oil.

When your home is already broken to bits
And the maternal "help yourself" comes no more from the
    tomb,
Dark kitchen, poverty of love.

XLIV

Este piano viaja para adentro,
viaja a saltos alegres.
Luego medita en ferrado reposo,
clavado con diez horizontes.

Adelanta. Arrástrase bajo túneles,
más allá, bajo túneles de dolor,
bajo vértebras que fugan naturalmente.

Otras veces van sus trompas,
lentas asias amarillas de vivir,
van de eclipse,
y se espulgan pesadillas insectiles,
ya muertas para el trueno, heraldo de los génesis.

Piano oscuro ¿a quién atisbas
con tu sordera que me oye,
con tu mudez que me asorda?
Oh pulso misterioso.

Trilce

LOS MINEROS

Los mineros salieron de la mina
remontando sus ruinas venideras,
fajaron su salud con estampidos
y, elaborando su función mental,
cerraron con sus voces
el socavón, en forma de síntoma profundo.

¡Era de ver sus polvos corrosivos!
¡Era de oír sus óxidos de altura!
Cuñas de boca, yunques de boca, aparatos de boca. (¡Es
formidable!)

X L I V

This piano travels within,
Travels in joyful leaps.
Then it meditates in ironbound repose,
Nailed by ten horizons.

It goes forward. It drags itself below tunnels,
Farther, below tunnels of pain,
Below vertebrae that, of course, take flight.

At other times its trumpets,
Slow yellow Asias of living,
Go into eclipse
And delouse themselves of insectile nightmares
Dead already from thunder, herald of genesis.

Dark piano, whom are you peeping at,
With your deafness that hears me,
With your muteness that deafens me?
O mysterious pulsation!

T H E   M I N E R S

The miners went forth from the mine,
Mounting its future ruins,
Attacking its health with gunshots,
And fashioning its function of the mind,
With their voices they closed
The cavern shaped like a profound symptom.

Their corrosive powder was something to see!
Their oxides of height were something to hear!
Wedges of mouths, anvils of mouths, instruments of mouths.
    (It is tremendous!)

El orden de sus túmulos,
sus inducciones plásticas, sus respuestas corales,
agolpáronse al pie de ígneos percances
y airente amarillura conocieron los trístidos y tristes,
imbuídos
del metal que se acaba, del metaloide pálido y pequeño.

Craneados de labor,
y en calzados de cuero de vizcacha,
calzados de senderos infinitos,
y los ojos de físico llorar,
creadores de la profundidad,
saben, a cielo intermitente de escalera,
bajar mirando para arriba,
saben subir mirando para abajo.

¡Loor al antiguo juego de su naturaleza,
a sus insomnes órganos, a su saliva rústica!
¡Crezcan la yerba, el liquen y la rana en sus adverbios!
¡Felpa de hierro a sus nupciales sábanas!
¡Mujeres hasta abajo, sus mujeres!
¡Mucha felicidad para los suyos!
¡Son algo portentoso, los mineros
remontando sus ruinas venideras;
elaborando su función mental
y abriendo con sus voces
el corazón, en forma de síntoma profundo!
¡Loor a su naturaleza amarillenta,
a su linterna mágica,
a sus cubos y rombos, a sus percances plásticos,
a sus ojazos de seis nervios ópticos
y a sus hijos que juegan en la Iglesia
y a sus tácitos padres infantiles!
¡Salud, oh creadores de la profundidad!

Poemas Humanos (1939)

The order of their tombs,
Their plastic persuasions, their choral responses,
Beat at the foot of igneous misfortunes
And the sad and saddened knew an airy yellowness
Infused
With finished metal, with metalloid small and pale.

Skulled with labor,
And shod with rodent leather,
Shod with infinite paths
And eyes of physical weeping,
Creators of profundity,
They know, in the intermittent sky of the mine lift,
How to descend looking upward,
How to rise looking downward.

Praise the ancient play of their nature,
Their sleepless organs, their rustic saliva!
Let grass grow, the lichen and the frog, in their adverbs!
Iron plush in their nuptial blankets!
Women, through and through, their women!
Much joy is theirs!
They are something portentous, the miners,
Mounting its future ruins,
Fashioning its function of the mind
And with their voices opening
The heart shaped like a profound symptom!
Praise their yellow nature,
Their magic lantern,
Its cubes and its rhomboids, its plastic misfortunes,
And their large eyes with six optic nerves
And their children who play in the Church
And their silent, childlike fathers!
Salud, O creators of profundity!

L A C O L E R A

La cólera que quiebra al hombre en niños,
que quiebra al niño en pájaros iguales,
y al pájaro, después, en huevecillos;
la cólera del pobre
tiene un aceite contra dos vinagres.

La cólera que al árbol quiebra en hojas,
a la hoja, en botones desiguales,
y al botón, en ranuras telescópicas;
la cólera del pobre
tiene dos ríos contra muchos mares.

La cólera que quiebra al bien en dudas,
a la duda, en tres arcos semejantes,
y al arco, luego, en tumbas imprevistas;
la cólera del pobre
tiene un acero contra dos puñales.

La cólera que quiebra al alma en cuerpos,
al cuerpo, en órganos desemejantes,
y al órgano, en octavos pensamientos;
la cólera del pobre
tiene un fuego central contra dos cráteres.

Poemas humanos

A N G E R

Anger that breaks a man into children,
That breaks the child into birds all alike,
And then the bird into little eggs;
The anger of the poor
Has an oil against two vinegars.

The anger that breaks the tree into leaves,
The leaf into unequal buds,
And the bud into telescopic grooves;
The anger of the poor
Has two rivers against many seas.

The anger that breaks the good into doubts
And the doubt into three similar arcs
And then the arc into unforeseen tombs;
The anger of the poor
Has a sword against two daggers.

The anger that breaks the soul into bodies
And the bodies into dissimilar organs
And the organ into octaves of thought;
The anger of the poor
Has a central fire against two craters.

LOS NUEVE MONSTRUOS

Y, desgraciadamente,
el dolor crece en el mundo a cada rato,
crece a treinta minutos por segundo, paso a paso,
y la naturaleza del dolor, es el dolor dos veces
y la condición del martirio, carnívora, voraz,
es el dolor, dos veces
y la función de la hierba purísima, el dolor
dos veces
y el bien de ser, dolernos doblemente.

Jamás, hombres humanos,
hubo tanto dolor en el pecho, en la solapa, en la cartera,
en el vaso, en la carnicería, en la aritmética!
Jamás tanto cariño doloroso,
jamás tan cerca arremetió lo lejos,
jamás el fuego nunca
jugó mejor su rol de frío muerto!
Jamás, señor ministro de salud, fué la salud
más mortal
y la migrana extrajo tanta frente de la frente!
Y el mueble tuvo en su cajón, dolor,
el corazón, en su cajón, dolor,
la lagartija, en su cajón, dolor.

Crece la desdicha, hermanos hombres,
más pronto que la máquina, a diez máquinas, y crece
con la res de Rousseau, con nuestras barbas;
crece el mal por razones que ignoramos
y es una inundación con propios líquidos,
con propio barro y propia nube sólida!
Invierte el sufrimiento posiciones, da función
en que el humor acuoso es vertical
al pavimento,
el ojo es visto y esta oreja oída,

THE NINE MONSTERS

And, unfortunately,
At each moment sorrow grows in the world,
It grows thirty minutes per second, step by step,
And the nature of sorrow is double sorrow
And the condition of martyrdom, carnivorous, voracious,
Is sorrow, double sorrow,
And the function of the purest grass, double
Sorrow
And the joy of living we suffer from doubly.

Never, O human beings,
Was there such sorrow in the breast, in the lapels, in the
    pocket flap,
In the glass, in the butcher shop, in arithmetic!
Never so much sorrowful tenderness,
Never did the distance attack so close at hand,
Never did fire play so well
Its role of icy death!
Never, O Minister of Health, was health
More deadly
Nor did the migraine pull so directly at the forehead!
And the furniture find sorrow in its chest,
The heart, sorrow in its chest,
The little lizard, sorrow in its chest.

Misery grows, O my brother men,
More quickly than the machine to ten machines, and grows
With the breed of Rousseau, with our beards;
Evil grows for reasons we do not know
And is a flood with its own liquids,
With its own clay and its own solid cloud!
Invert the positions of suffering, make it come about
That the aqueous humor is vertical
To the pavement,
And the eye is seen and this ear is heard

y esta oreja da nueve campanadas a la hora
del rayo, y nueve carcajadas
a la hora del trigo, y nueve sones hembras
a la hora del llanto, y nueve cánticos
a la hora del hambre, y nueve truenos
y nueve látigos, menos un grito.

El dolor nos agarra, hermanos hombres,
por detrás, de perfil,
y nos coloca en los cinemas,
nos clava en los gramófonos,
nos desclava en los pechos, cae perpendicularmente
a nuestros boletos, a nuestras cartas;
y es muy grave sufrir, puede uno orar.
Pues de resultas
del dolor, hay algunos
que nacen, otros crecen, otros mueren,
y otros que nacen y no mueren, y otros
que no nacen ni mueren. (Son los más.)
Y también de resultas
del sufrimiento, estoy triste
hasta la cabeza, y más triste hasta el tobillo,
de ver el pan, crucificado, al nabo,
ensangrentado,
llorando, a la cebolla,
al cereal, en general, harina,
a la sal, hecho polvo, al agua, huyendo,
al vino, un ecce-homo,
tan pálida a la nieve, al sol tan árido!

Cómo, hermanos humanos,
no deciros que ya no puedo y
ya no puedo con tanto cajón,
tanto minuto, tanta
lagartija y tanta
inversión, tanto lejos y tanta sed de sed!
Señor ministro de salud; ¿qué hacer?

And this ear immediately gives forth nine bell strokes
From the light ray and immediately nine bursts of laughter
From the wheat and immediately nine female sounds
From weeping and immediately nine chants
From hunger and nine thunders
And nine lashes less a cry.

Sorrow claws us, brother men,
From behind, in profile,
And seats us in the cinema,
Nails us in the phonographs,
Draws out the nails in our breast, falls perpendicularly
On our tickets, upon our letters;
And as the suffering is very intense, one can pray.
Then, as a result of
Sorrow, there are some
Who are born, others grow, others die,
And others who are born and do not die and others
Who are neither born nor die. (These are the majority.)
And likewise, as a result
Of suffering, I am sad
Up to my head and sadder yet down to my ankles
To see the bread crucified, the turnip
Bloody,
The onion weeping,
The cereal, generally, the flour,
The salt, turned into dust, the water fleeing,
The wine an *ecce homo*,
The snow so pale, the sun so dry.

How, O brother humans,
To avoid telling you that already I cannot endure
And already I cannot endure so many chests,
So many minutes, so many
Little lizards and so many
Inversions, so many distances, and so much thirst for thirst!
O Minister of Health: What can we do?

Ah, desgraciadamente, hombres humanos,
hay, hermanos, muchísimo que hacer.

Poemas humanos

PEDRO ROJAS

Solía escribir con su dedo grande en el aire:
"¡Viban los compañeros! Pedro Rojas,"
de Miranda del Ebro, padre y hombre,
marido y hombre, ferroviario y hombre,
padre y más hombre, Pedro y sus dos muertes.

Papel de viento, lo han matado: ¡pasa!
Pluma de carne, lo han matado: ¡pasa!
¡Abisa a todos los compañeros, pronto!

Palo en el que han colgado su madero,
lo han matado;
¡lo han matado al pie de su dedo grande!
¡Han matado, a la vez, a Pedro, a Rojas!

¡Viban los compañeros
a la cabecera de su aire escrito!
¡Viban con esta b del buitre en las entrañas
de Pedro
y de Rojas, del héroe y del mártir!

Registrándole, muerto, sorprendiéronle
en su cuerpo un gran cuerpo, para
el alma del mundo,
y en la chaqueta una cuchara muerta.

Pedro también solía comer
entre las criaturas de su carne, asear, pintar
la mesa y vivir dulcemente
en representación de todo el mundo,

Ah, unfortunately, human beings
There are, O brothers, so many many things to do.

PEDRO ROJAS

He used to write in the air with his forefinger
"Long live the comrades! Pedro Rojas,"
Of Miranda del Ebro, father and man,
Husband and man, railworker and man,
Father and still more man, Pedro and his two deaths.

Paper in the wind, they have killed him: pass on!
Feather of flesh, they have killed him: pass on!
Quickly announce it to all the comrades!

Post on which they hung the wood of him,
They have killed him;
They have killed him at the foot of his forefinger!
They have killed both Pedro and Rojas at the same time!

Long live the comrades,
Written at the top of his air!
Hurrah for them with this v of the vulture in the bowels
Of Pedro
And of Rojas, of the hero and the martyr!

Searching him dead, they found
A great body in his body, fit
For the soul of the world,
And in his coat a dead spoon.

Pedro, moreover, used to eat
Among the children of his flesh, to polish and paint
The table and live gently,
Representing all the world,

y esta cuchara anduvo en su chaqueta,
despierto o bien cuando dormía, siempre,
cuchara muerta viva, ella y sus símbolos.
¡Abisa a todos los compañeros, pronto!
¡Viban los compañeros al pie de esta cuchara para siempre!

Lo han matado, obligándole a morir
a Pedro, a Rojas, al obrero, al hombre, a aquél
que nació muy niñín, mirando al cielo,
y que luego creció, se puso rojo
y luchó con sus células, sus nos, sus todavías, sus hambres,
    sus pedazos.
Lo han matado suavemente
entre el cabello de su mujer, la Juana Vásquez,
a la hora del fuego, al año del balazo
y cuando andaba cerca ya de todo.

Pedro Rojas, así, después de muerto,
se levantó, besó su catafalco ensangrentado,
lloró por España
y volvió a escribir con el dedo en el aire:
"¡Viban los compañeros! Pedro Rojas."
Su cadáver estaba lleno de mundo.

España, aparta de mí este cáliz (1940)

And this spoon traveled in his coat
Always awake, even when he slept,
Spoon, dead while alive, it and its symbols.
Quickly announce it to all the comrades!
Long live the comrades at the foot of this spoon forever!

They have killed him, forcing him to die,
Pedro, Rojas, the worker, the man, he
Who was born very little, looking at the sky,
And when he grew became red
And struggled with his cells, his "noes," his "and yets," his
    hungers, his fragments.
They have killed him smoothly
In the hair of his wife, Juana Vásquez,
At the moment of firing, in the year of the bullet,
And when he walked close to everything.

So Pedro Rojas, after death
Rose up, kissed his bloody catafalque,
Wept for Spain
And came back to write with his finger in the air:
"Long live the comrades! Pedro Rojas."
His body was full of the world.

PEQUEÑO RESPONSO A UN HEROE DE LA REPUBLICA

Un libro quedó al borde de su cintura muerta,
un libro retoñaba de su cadáver muerto.
Se llevaron al héroe,
y corpórea y aciaga entró su boca en nuestro aliento;
sudamos todos, el ombligo a cuestas;
caminantes las lunas nos seguían;
también sudaba de tristeza el muerto.

Y un libro, en la batalla de Toledo,
un libro, atrás un libro, arriba un libro, retoñaba del cadáver.

Poesía del pómulo morado, entre el decirlo
y el callarlo,
poesía en la carta moral que acompañara
a su corazón.
Quedóse el libro y nada más, que no hay
insectos en la tumba,
y quedó al borde de su manga el aire remojándose
y haciéndose gaseoso, infinito.

Todos sudamos, el ombligo a cuestas,
también sudaba de tristeza el muerto
y un libro, yo lo ví sentidamente,
un libro, atrás un libro, arriba un libro
retoñó del cadáver exabrupto.

España, aparta de mí este cáliz

LITTLE RESPONSORY FOR A
REPUBLICAN HERO

A book lay beside his dead belt,
A book was sprouting from his dead body.
They raised the hero
And, corporeal and sad, his mouth entered our breath.
We were all sweating, dog tired,
As we traveled the moons were following us;
And the dead man, too, was sweating with sadness.

And a book, in the battle of Toledo,
A book, a book behind, a book above, was sprouting from
    the corpse.

Poetry of the purple cheek, between reciting it
And keeping it silent,
Poetry in the moral letter that accompanied
His heart.
The book remained and nothing more, since there are
No insects in the tomb
And the air under the edge of his sleeve continued to grow
    moist
And to become gaseous, infinite.

We were all sweating, dog tired,
And the dead man, too, was sweating with sadness.
And a book, I saw it, feeling it,
A book behind, a book above,
Sprouted from the violent corpse.

MASA

Al fin de la batalla,
y muerto el combatiente, vino hacia él un hombre
y le dijo: "¡No mueras; te amo tanto!"
Pero el cadáver ¡ay!, siguió muriendo.

Se le acercaron dos y repitiéronle:
"¡No nos dejes! ¡Valor! ¡Vuelve a la vida!"
Pero el cadáver ¡ay!, siguió muriendo.

Acudieron a él veinte, cien, mil, quinientos mil,
clamando: "¡Tanto amor, y no poder nada contra la muerte!"
Pero el cadáver ¡ay!, siguió muriendo.

Le rodearon millones de individuos,
con un ruego común: "¡Quédate hermano!"
Pero el cadáver ¡ay!, siguió muriendo.

Entonces, todos los hombres de la tierra
le rodearon; les vió el cadáver triste, emocionado;
incorporóse lentamente,
abrazó al primer hombre; echóse a andar . . .

España, aparta de mí este cáliz

MASSES

At the end of the battle,
When the fighter was dead, a man came toward him
And said to him "Do not die, I love you so!"
But the corpse, alas, went on dying!

Then two approached him and repeated it,
"Do not leave us! Courage! Come back to life!"
But the corpse, alas, went on dying.

Then twenty came, a hundred, a thousand, five hundred
     thousand,
Clamoring, "So much love and nothing can be done about
     death!"
But the corpse, alas, went on dying.

Millions of individuals surrounded him,
With a common entreaty, "Stay with us, brother!"
But the corpse, alas, went on dying.

Then all the men of the earth
Surrounded him; the corpse looked at them sadly, full of
     emotion;
Sat up slowly,
Embraced the first man; and began to walk . . .

JACINTO FOMBONA
PACHANO

b. 1901, Caracas, Venezuela

JACINTO FOMBONA
PACHANO

b. 1901, Caracas, Venezuela

FOMBONA PACHANO is outstanding among the younger Venezuelan poets. Like so many Spanish American writers, he, too, serves the government of his country. He is descended from a literary family and studied political science in the Central University of Venezuela. After his book, *Virajes,* was published he was elected to the Venezuelan Academy. He has acted as secretary general to the State of Monegas, was a member of the Venezuelan Embassy in Washington from 1936 to 1940, and now is serving as secretary general to the State of Miranda, Venezuela. He has been a contributor to the publication *Viernes,* around which are grouped the most active members of the younger generation of Venezuelan poets. Fombona's first important book, *Virajes,* is remarkable for its fresh, idyllic quality. It contains poems on simple genre themes and also a whole section of *corridos* making use of local legends. Much of this book is definitely indigenist. On the whole, Fombona Pachano's early poetry stamps him as a romantic nationalist of great charm. His most recent work, *Las torres desprevenidas,* written while he was in Washington, indicates a new phase in his development and a much broader point of view. The war has moved him to attempt more ambitious themes. In this book he uses brilliant associative imagery which owes something to surrealism. The recent poems are full of pity and terror—expressing the tragedy of the war's innocent victims and celebrating man's aspirations toward a better world.

"La queja" is particularly interesting as a specimen of indigenism. It is the first in a series of seven *corríos* (or *corridos*), poems written in the folk form, which deal with the life of Santos Zárate, a mythical folk character (Indian or mestizo) who was something of a revolutionary hero. Fombona Pachano traces the career and tragic death of this character in allusive and symbolic style. He has apparently made original contributions to the legend. The whole series of poems constitutes a miniature folk epic.

El canto del hijo. Caracas, 1926.
Virajes. Caracas, 1932.
Las torres desprevenidas. Caracas, 1940.

LA COCA

—Vámos! Hay tiempo todavía
para alcanzar al día
en el andén . . .
Vuela! Desesperada y loca,
en su silbato, la coca
silba:
      —Pasajeros, al tren! . . .

—Pero,
¿en dónde está el sendero
de la estación?

—Allá, tras de los árboles, en donde sus baúles azules
está cerrando el día . . .
Oye silbar la coca con desesperación . . .
Vámos allá, que hay tiempo todavía! . . .

—Quedémonos, mejor, bajo la fronda,
no podremos llegar;
ya el silbato se ahonda
y se aleja, se aleja sin parar.

—Ya entraron en el túnel de las estrellas! . . .

—Y vas a llorar, lo presumo,
porque otra vez se nos escapa el día!
Tienes razón . . . de tantas cosas bellas
quedar tan sólo esa gasa de humo
que pinta el sol sobre la lejanía! . . .

—Oye silbar la coca . . . Oye marcharse el día . . .

                           Virajes (1932)

THE COCA TREE

"Let's go! we have still time
To catch up with the day
At the station platform . . .
Fly! Mad and desperate,
The coca tree whistles
On its whistle:
　　　　　All aboard! . . ."

"But
Where is the path
To the station?"

"Yonder, through the trees where the sky
Is locking its blue trunks up . . .
Hear the coca tree whistle desperately . . .
Let's go, there is still time! . . ."

"Better to stay here under the leaves,
We can't make it;
Already the whistle deepens
And moves off, moves off without waiting."

"Already they are entering the tunnel of the stars! . . ."

"And you are going to weep, I suppose,
Because the day has escaped us once more!
You're right . . . from so many beautiful things
This cloud of smoke the sun paints over the distances
Is all that is left! . . ."

"Hear the coca tree whistling . . . hear the day depart-
　　ing . . ."

E L   P O Z O

En el suelo agrietado
del patio familiar, la lluvia un pozo
de cristalinas aguas ha estancado,

donde en rebelde y bravo desaliño,
sus naves de papel, con alborozo,
cargadas de ilusión, esparce un niño;

donde el azul celaje,
la clara nube y la lejana estrella,
detienen, al pasar, su largo viaje;

donde la tarde eclógica de mayo
ve en el limpio cristal cómo destella,
en un postrer fulgor, su último rayo;

donde, en inquieta confusión el ave,
al mirar el azul bajo sus alas,
a qué cielo volar, ya no lo sabe;

donde, en sereno y armonioso giro,
sobre la onda, en trémulas escalas,
la brisa al resbalar deja un suspiro;

y en cuyo seno luminoso y hondo,
tras el buceo de una dicha ignota,
se hunden las pupilas hasta el fondo,

mientras que sube, en misterioso anhelo,
un diáfano vapor de cada gota
a convertirse en lágrima del cielo! . . .

Pero mañana el sol, el despiadado
sol de mañana, ha de venir, Dios mío!
para secar el pozo abandonado . . .

THE PUDDLE

In the rutted soil of the household patio
The rain has collected
In a puddle of crystalline water,

Where a child gaily scatters
His paper boats, freighted with illusion,
In brave and rebellious disorder;

Where the blue sky-patterns,
Where the bright cloud and distant star
In passing interrupt their long voyage;

Where the idyllic afternoon of May
Sees its last glimmer, its final ray,
In the crystal clear as a star.

Where the bird, in inquiet confusion,
Seeing the blue below his wings,
Knows not which sky to fly toward;

Where, in serene and harmonious gyrations,
The breeze leaves a sigh as it glides
On the wave in quivering scales;

Where the pupil sinks into the depths
Of its profound and luminous bosom,
Diving for unknown joy;

While, mysterious, desirous,
From each drop a diaphanous vapor arises
To turn into the tears of the sky! . . .

But tomorrow the sun, the pitiless
Morning sun must come, ah me!
To dry up the abandoned puddle . . .

y bajo el sol de fuego,
el claro pozo quedará vacío
con la perfecta inexpresión de un ciego! . . .

Virajes

MAÑANA, COMO ES
DOMINGO

Con la cartilla en el brazo
volverás muy bien sabido,
y te vestirán de nuevo,
mañana, como es domingo . . .
Como es domingo, mañana,
los dos iremos al circo,
donde colgó su trapecio
la araña, del arbolito,
donde se traga el cocuyo
todo un tizón encendido,
y la hormiguita levanta
su arena de muchos kilos,
y el gusanito de monte
se descoyunta y da brincos.
Como es domingo, mañana,
los dos iremos al circo.

Qué bueno es saber las letras
cuando mañana es domingo!,
para estrenar como el alba
calzones de blanco lino
y cuello azul con encaje
del que se ponen los ríos.
Si quieres saber la cara
que ha de enseñarte el domingo,
si está de luto o de fiesta,
vente al estanque conmigo,
y, si te ríe, es seguro
que iremos con él al circo.

And beneath the fiery sun
The clear pool will be left empty,
Like one blind, completely devoid of expression! . . .

S I N C E   T O M O R R O W   I S   S U N D A Y

With your A B C book under your arm
You'll come back knowing your lessons,
And they will put your new clothes on
Tomorrow, because it is Sunday . . .
Since it is Sunday tomorrow,
We two shall go to the circus
Where the spider hung his trapeze
From the sapling,
Where the glowworm swallows
The whole of a glowing ember,
Where the little ant lifts up
His many-pound grain of sand,
And the mountain caterpillar
Throws out his joints and does high jumps.
Since it is Sunday tomorrow,
We two shall go to the circus.

How nice to know your letters
When tomorrow is Sunday!
To wear, like the daybreak,
White linen trousers
And a blue collar with lace on it
Like that which is worn by the rivers.
And if you would know what face
Sunday is going to show you,
Whether it's mournful or festive,
Come to the pond with me,
If it laughs at you, it is certain
We shall go with it to the circus.

Mas, pudiera estar de luto,
porque es muchacho el domingo
que tiene un dómine serio
que se llama San Isidro.
Vamos los dos a pedirle
que no lo ponga en castigo:
patrón del sol y del agua,
cajero de campesinos,
manto de siete colores
con mil agujas cosido,
y auroras en el sombrero,
como luce en sus dominios.
Vamos los dos a pedirle:
patroncito,
abre la puerta del aula
para que no esté sombrío,
y el viento seque las ropas
azules de tu pupilo;
y del tesoro que guardas,
además, como eres rico,
pónle monedas de soles,
de soles en los bolsillos,
que hoy nadie labra las tierras
y vamos todos al circo,
saltando el cielo en los pozos
que iluminan los caminos.

Qué bueno es saber las letras
cuando mañana es domingo! . . .

Virajes

But it could be mournful
Because Sunday is a fellow
Who has a serious teacher
Who is called Saint Isidro.
Let us both go to ask him
Not to punish Sunday:
Patron of sun and water
Treasurer of the farmers,
With mantle of seven colors
Sewed with a thousand needles
And with dawns in his hat,
So he dresses in his dominions.
Let us both go to ask him:
Little patron,
Open the door of the classroom
So he won't have a gloomy face
And so that the wind may dry out
The blue garments of your pupil;
And of the treasure you're keeping,
Since you are a rich man,
Give him coins of sun besides,
Coins of sun in his pockets,
For today no one works in the fields
And we all go to the circus,
Skipping the sky in the puddles
That light up the roadways.

How nice to know your letters
When tomorrow is Sunday! . . .

LA QUEJA

Dáme un romance, Orinoco,
Apure, dáme un corrío,
mi Guaire, dáme una copla,
para cantar lo que digo.

Para cantar lo que digo,
con luna donde se vea,
como el samán de la orilla,
como la nube viajera.

Como la nube viajera,
como la tarde y el viento,
como la quilla del bongo
que va pulsando luceros.

Que va pulsando luceros
de Apures y de Orinocos;
mi Guaire ha tiempo discurre
con la nostalgia de un bongo.

Con la nostalgia de un bongo
para las cuerdas del Guaire:
Apure, dáme un corrío,
dáme, Orinoco, un romance.

Dáme, Orinoco, un romance,
porque tiene el indio Santos,
de tu albedrío, el impulso,
de tu creciente, el caballo.

De tu creciente, el caballo,
como del Apure tiene
los bríos con que desnuda
la lanza que te enfurece.

THE COMPLAINT

Orinoco, give me a *romance*,*
Apuret, give me a folk song,
My Guairet, give me a ballad
In order to sing what I say.

In order to sing what I say,
Wherever the moon can be seen,
Like the rain tree on the shore,
Like the voyaging cloud.

Like the voyaging cloud,
Like the wind and the twilight,
And like the keel of the canoe
That goes on pulsing bright stars.

That goes on pulsing bright stars
Of Apures and Orinocos;
My Guaire has long been flowing
With a canoe's nostalgia.

With a canoe's nostalgia
For the cords of the Guaire:
Apure, give me a folk song,
Orinoco, give me a *romance*.

Orinoco, give me a *romance*
Since the Indian, Santos, possesses
The power of your free will
The horse of your overflowing.

The horse of your overflowing,
As he draws from the Apure
The vigor with which he bares
The lance that drives you to fury.

* The *romance* is a Spanish popular poetic form with an eight-syllable line.
† The Apure and the Guaire are both Venezuelan rivers.

La lanza que te enfurece!
Sólo me sirves, mi Guaire,
para una queja de amores
de la mestiza de Zárate.

De la mestiza de Zárate:
—Deja esta vida de muerte! . . .
Un ángel besa en la brisa
las palmas de los caneyes.

Las palmas de los caneyes:
Por la Victoria y por Cagua,
un potro color de azufre
todas las noches cabalga.

Virajes

MI AMERICA, LA DULCE

Tú venías vestida de guitarras y pájaros
y tu sombrero era de sol y tiernas palmas,
cuando de pronto me dijeron
que vientos encendidos te buscaban
para soplar tizones en tu falda.

Volé. Te ví los lazos verdes
y el cinturón de agua,
te ví el traje, las flores y toqué tu sombrero.
Y pensé que la vida estaba intacta,
que tú, mi dulce América, no ardías.

Y, sin embargo, yo el inquieto,
yo el que canta en las albas, yo el reloj de la cómoda,
yo el que interrumpe el sueño de los hartos,
sé que es verdad y te digo: despierta!
porque he oído las lenguas de fuego en los pasillos,
porque ya están crujiendo tus guitarras tostadas,
a ese negro rescoldo que les raja las fibras,

The lance which drives you to fury!
You only serve me, my Guaire,
As a lover's complaint
For the half-breed woman of Zárate.

For the half-breed woman of Zárate:
—She is leaving this life of dying! . . .
In the breeze an angel kisses
The palm leaves of the huts.

The palm leaves of the huts:
Through Victoria and through Cagua,
A colt the color of sulphur
Goes galloping every night.

AMERICA, MY SWEET

You came dressed in birds and guitars
And your hat was of sun and tender palm leaves
When they suddenly told me
That flaming winds were seeking you
To blow up embers in your lap.

I flew. I saw your green bowknots
And your girdle of water,
I saw your garment, the flowers, and I touched your hat.
And I thought that life was still inviolate
Since you, my sweet America, were not burning.

And yet I, the unquiet one,
I who sing in the dawns, I, the clock on the bureau,
I who interrupt the sleep of the self-satisfied,
Know that it is true and I say to you: awaken!
For I have heard the tongues of fire in the passages,
For your scorched guitars are already crackling
From those black embers that split their fibers

cuando para dormir cuelgas el traje
en el ropero de tus siestas.

No hay que dormir. Véla en la piedra,
véla en la pluma y en la onda,
en la semilla y el retoño, véla,
en el pan, en el aire,
en la llama de la esquila que tiembla
borrando y alumbrando terrores del espejo.

Vé que a ninguno falte
ni la aguja ni el hilo para zurcir su casa,
ni el agua de amellar filos al rojo,
ni el corazón, ni las abejas,
ni el vellón y la leche de los mansos.

Vé que en todos los techos haya humo
y haya canción en cada hoguera,
que rían todas las ventanas
y que todas las puertas quiebren
las llaves espantosas.

Quiero salvarte. Quiero
que no te alcancen con sus lenguas,
que no te tiznen esos gritos
que andan rayando túnicas de corderos y niños.
A ti, mi nueva, a ti, mi dulce,
sin cerrojo en tu casa, sin limón en tu plato,
la inocente, la mía,
quiero salvarte yo, quiero salvarte,
verte seguir intacta,
segura para siempre de tus pies y tus manos,
sobre puentes sin riesgo,
con la rosa de todos los vientos en tu boca,
vestida para todos de guitarras y pájaros.

Las torres desprevenidas (1940)

When you hang up your gown at bedtime
In the wardrobe of your slumbers.

You must not sleep. Keep watch in the stone,
Keep watch in the wave and in the feather,
In the seed and in the seedling, keep your vigil,
In the air and in the breadloaf,
In the call of the bell that trembles,
Obscuring and illuminating terrors of the mirror.

See to it that no one lacks
Either the needle or the thread to sew his house up,
Either the water for tempering red-hot blades,
Either the heart or the bees,
Or the fleece and the milk of the bellwethers.

See to it that over all the roofs there is smoke
And that there is song at each hearthstone,
That all the windows are laughing
And that all the doors fracture
The fearful keys.

I want to save you. I do not want them
With those tongues of theirs to reach you,
I do not want those cries to scorch you,
Those cries that go streaking the robes of lambs and of chil-
    dren.
You are new, my sweet,
Without a latch in your house, without a lemon in your dish,
O innocent and mine,
I want to save you, I, I want to save you,
I want to see you continue inviolate,
Your hands and feet, forever secure
Upon safe bridges,
With the rose of all the winds in your mouth,
Dressed for everyone in birds and guitars.

YA LAS NUBES ME LO
TENIAN DICHO

La edición de la tarde
sale vestida de sirenas.
Y una alondra de ceniza es una aldea quemada,
con pastores, con flautas y campanas,
rebaños y niños de humo,
una aldea de un mapa que han perdido mis dedos
y que la nube se encontró
para lloverlo en cualquier parte.

Qué bandadas de pájaros en llamas
me nublan el sol y están cayendo en nuestros techos.
Qué aldeas por el aire.
Qué buches incendiados lloran plumas dispersas,
al norte, al sur, matando los jardines,
avasallando todos los alientos,
silenciando las plumas verdaderas.

Los negros titulares quieren que yo los compre:
me los ofrece un ángel sin zapatos,
un obrero sin manos.
Y antes he visto
apagarme los verdes y cerrar mis ventanas
las tres alondras de ceniza
que volaron anoche hacia mi casa.

Yo amaba esas aldeas caídas del micrófono,
por las que me detuve tantas veces
en mis viajes del muro con el índice.
Pero mis labios ya no saben
dónde colocar sus nombres. Y tendré para enterrarlas
que buscar entre remiendos, entre paredes con lepra,
entre sábanas con sangre,
el cementerio de los mapas.

THE CLOUDS HAVE ALREADY TOLD ME

The evening edition
Comes out dressed in sirens.
A burnt village is a skylark made of ashes
With shepherds, with flutes and bells,
Flocks and children of smoke,
A village from a map my fingers have lost,
With which the cloud has collided
To shower it elsewhere as rain.

What flocks of birds all flaming
Cloud over my sun and are falling upon our roofs!
What villages in the air!
What breasts of birds on fire weep scattered feathers
To the north, to the south, killing the gardens,
Subduing every breath,
Silencing the real feathers!

The black headlines want me to buy them:
A barefoot angel offers them to me,
A worker with no hands.
And I have already seen
The three skylarks made of ashes
That flew toward my house last night,
Snuffing out the foliage and closing my windows.

I was a lover of those villages fallen from the microphone
Where I paused so many times
As my index finger traveled over the wall.
But my lips no longer know
Where to put their names. And to bury them I shall have to
Look among bloody patches, among leprous walls,
Among bloody sheets
For the cemetery of the maps.

El que incendia una alondra, el que mata una aldea,
vuelve ciegos sus dedos y hace horribles sus ojos,
porque ya nunca más podrá encontrarla
sino en su piel más fría que roa el diente del gusano.

Yo no puedo mirar las nubes,
tú no puedes mirar las nubes,
nadie puede mirarlas como las vimos antes,
porque en ellas hay hogueras con criaturas encendidas,
y lo que llueve en nuestros campos
es humo de organillos y de niños,
lana dulce de ovejas y de flautas quemadas.

No hay que vender la muerte de las alondras,
ni gritarla por boca de los ángeles
en esquinas y plazas.
No hay que dar esas manos de palo a los mendigos
ni ese almíbar de horror a los insectos.

No hay que engordar con eso.
Ya sabéis lo que pasa al asesino.
No vengáis a decirme cómo murió la aldea,
cómo suena una carne de campanas al rojo
ni un corazón en brasas.

Sé más que vuestro grito,
que vuestro falso grito de tinta por las calles.

Las torres desprevenidas

He who burns a skylark, he who kills a village
Blinds his fingers and makes his eyes horrible,
For never more shall he find it
Save in his icy skin gnawed by the tooth of the worm.

I cannot look at the clouds,
You cannot look at the clouds,
No one can look at the clouds as they formerly looked at
    them,
For there are bonfires in them with creatures in flames
And what rains on our fields
Is the smoke of hand organs and children,
Sweet wool of sheep and burnt flutes.

There is no need to sell the death of skylarks
Nor to cry it with the mouths of angels
On squares and street corners.
There is no need to give those wooden hands to the beggars
Nor that sirup of horror to the insects.

There is no need to get fat on it.
You already know what happens to the assassin.
Do not come to tell me how the village died,
How a red-hot flesh of bells
Or a heart in embers sounds.

I know more than your shouting,
Than your false inky shouting in the streets.

DANZA DE LA LLAVE
PERDIDA

Por el mar, apagando
vuestra cola de ajenjo y de ceniza,
entre ondinas de humo donde danza la muerte,
venís, llegáis vosotras,
las reinas por carbones de alfiles negros desterradas,
las reinas amarillas sin cuadro en el tablero.

Y detrás de las reinas,
venís, llegáis también vosotros,
pobres caballos sin cabeza,
pobres peones ácidos de triturar terrores con los dientes,
que ayer danzasteis para ellas
y ahora colgáis vuestros escudos
en la tienda del circo
o en la garganta del micrófono.

Venís, llegáis, danzando,
bajo inventadas lunas de frambuesa y de menta,
por donde os miro huyendo del aplauso y la risa,
mezclando en vuestra copa
los efímeros pétalos y los hollines insondables.

Por más que lo gritéis con tinta y luz en los carteles
no sois, no fuisteis de marfil;
fuisteis y sois de sangre, sois
de quinina o de sal o de limón, apenas.
Y tenéis que seguir danzando, danzando para todos,
y tenéis que recoger miga por miga vuestro azúcar.

El pie ya no os encaja en los relojes:
habéis perdido hasta la playa del próximo segundo,
se os ha roto la flecha de tanto azar previsto,
la campana de los manteles y las plumas.

DANCE OF THE LOST KEY

Through the sea,
Quenching your train of absinthe and ashes,
Among sea nymphs of smoke where death dances,
You come, you arrive,
Queens, exiled through coals of black bishops,
Yellow queens with no square on the chessboard.

And behind the queens,
You come, you, too, arrive,
Poor headless knights,
Poor pawns, soured from chewing terror with your teeth,
You, who used to dance for them,
And now you hang up your shields
In the tent in the arena
Or in the throat of the microphone.

You come, you arrive dancing
Beneath imaginary moons of mint and strawberry,
Whither I see you flying from the applause and the laughter,
Mixing within your cup
The ephemeral petals and unfathomable soots.

However much you cry out with color and light in the hand-
    bills,
You are not, you were not of marble;
You were and you are of blood, you are
Scarcely of quinine or of salt or of lemon.
And you have to go on dancing, dancing for everyone,
And you have to gather your sugar crumb by crumb.

Your foot does not fit into the watches:
You have lost even the shore of the last second,
The arrow of so much hoped-for luck is broken,
The bell of the tablecloths and the feathers.

Por eso andáis sin hora en el programa,
sin párpados ni boca para el sueño y el hambre,
vosotros, ay, las reinas amarillas,
los caballos y los peones,
que os coméis vuestro plato favorito
de coronas y cetros
ante mesas hundidas sin libreas ni patas
y dormís en el aire bajo puentes de avispas.

Ya os estarán mordiendo,
rojas o verdes, esas lunas, detrás de sus caretas;
ya os estará quemando
su llaga de moneda leprosa en vuestras albas,
porque vosotros ya contáis entre los ángeles
de alas caídas y tostadas
que les ponen su falsa sonrisa a las esquinas
bajo las lunas verdaderas.

Venís, llegáis danzando,
siempre danzando, porque vuestra llave,
la de abrir los dragones de la despensa y la bodega,
la llave dócil que han perdido vuestros dedos,
tendréis ahora que buscarla, por plazas y avenidas,
entre las madrugadas con tinta de los ángeles.

Las torres desprevenidas

Therefore you go without time on the program,
Without eyelids or mouth for sleep or hunger,
You, alas, the yellow queens,
The knights and the pawns,
Who eat your favorite dish
Of crowns and scepters
At sunken tables without servants or legs
And sleep in the air beneath bridges of wasps.

And already they will be gnawing you,
Those moons of red or green, behind their masks;
Already their ulcer of leprous money
Will be burning in your white robe,
For you are already counted among the angels,
With wings singed and fallen.
Who assume their false smile for the street corners
Beneath moons of reality.

You come, you arrive dancing,
Always dancing, because your key,
Which opens the dragons of the pantry and the wine cellar,
The docile key which your fingers have lost,
You have to seek now in squares and avenues,
Among dawns with the color of the angels.

ANUNCIO EL REINO DE LA ESTRELLA

Y ahora diré mi palabra para los hombres apacibles,
para los hombres que agonizan en silencio,
los que aun silabean el sentido del árbol,
del cordero y del niño, de la techumbre y la campana:

Hay un sitio en el mundo, hermanos míos,
hay un sitio en el mundo detrás de los incendios.
Mas allá del inútil ramillete de las granadas,
más allá de los garfios, de los filos, de las corazas y las redes,
a espaldas del carbón y la ceniza,
de las mejillas de papel y de los huesos machacados,
para la flor, la espiga, el vellón y la leche,
para todas las madres sin rencor en el mundo,
para el panal, tiene que haber un sitio.

Por encima del humo, por encima de hospitales y cuervos,
si salváis la muralla de alaridos y hedores,
si rompéis la gangrena que os apresa en el aire,
del otro lado, hermanos, bajo cielos inermes,
entre prados de sombra dulce, con altas nubes de agua alegre,
besan mares de ovejas, algún sitio en el mundo.

No preguntéis, no preguntéis: ¿en dónde?
Mirad primero vuestras uñas, vuestras mandíbulas,
si guadañas y sierras no están creciendo de vosotros,
si boca y manos tienen sabor de lana y lirio,
si hay seña en vuestros dedos de mariposas extinguidas,
de campanas muertas y cigarras mudas.

Id por la miel primero, por la miel más profunda,
más jocunda, que os ata el corazón a las abejas.

I ANNOUNCE THE KINGDOM
OF THE STAR

And now I shall speak my word to the men of peace,
To the men who suffer in silence,
To those who still utter the feelings of the tree,
Of the lamb and of the child, of the roof and the bell.

There is a place in the world, my brothers,
There is a place in the world beyond the burnings.
Further than the useless nosegay of the grenades,
Further than the hooks, the blades, the armor plate, and the
    nets,
Behind carbon and ashes,
Behind paper cheeks and crushed bones,
For the flower, the wheatear, the fleece, and the milk,
For all the rancorless mothers in the world,
For the honeycomb, there has to be a place.

Over the smoke, over the hospitals and ravens,
If you pass the rampart of stenches and screams,
If you pierce the gangrene that seizes you in the air,
On the other side, brothers, under unarmed skies,
Among fields of sweet shadow with high clouds of joyful
    water,
Seas of sheep kiss a certain place in the world.

Do not ask, oh, do not ask: Where is it?
Look first at your nails, your jaws, to see
Whether scythes and saws do not grow out of them,
Whether mouth and hands have the savor of wool and lily,
Whether on your fingers there are signs of extinguished
    butterflies,
Dead bells and mute cicadas.

Go for the first honey, the most profound,
The gayest, which joins your heart to the bees.

Mirad si en cada pecho se están copiando las estrellas,
si a su margen sin miedo puede asomarse un niño,
una flauta, un tejado, un palomar entero, sin borrarse.

Decidme qué habéis hecho con el fuego,
qué habéis hecho con el aire de los jardines y los pájaros,
con tanta oliva de mar como hundieron vuestros barcos,
con tanta tierra encinta de primaveras desdichadas.

Decidme qué moneda de sudor o de llanto
muere en vuestros bolsillos o es sangre en vuestros dientes.

Y si de veras sois los apacibles,
si sois de veras nardo y lino y vais desnudos,
entonces sabréis, entonces, que hay un sitio en el mundo,
un sitio, sí, que está naciendo de vuestra luz más limpia,
un sitio donde las hogueras forjan los cielos castos,
donde el aire engarza anillos de perfumes contentos,
donde el agua entre dos costas tiende lazos de tibios nudos,
donde la tierra es madre de mejillas y besos.

Si lo queréis vosotros, hay un sitio en el mundo,
hay un sitio en el mundo detrás de los incendios,
más allá de los vientres grávidos que os imploran,
por sus grietas de cementerios mutilados,
el reino blanco y dulce de la estrella.

Las torres desprevenidas

Look to see if in each breast the stars are duplicating them-
    selves
And if from their margins a child may peep in without fear,
Or a flute, a roof, an entire dovecote, without being effaced.

Tell me what you have done with fire,
What you have done with the garden air and the birds,
With so much olive of sea as your ships have sunk,
With so much earth, pregnant with unhappy springtimes.

Tell me what coin of sweat or of tears
Dies in your pockets or is blood on your teeth.

And if you are truly the men of peace
And if you are truly nard and linen and go naked,
Then, oh then you will know that there is a place in the
    world,
A place, indeed, that is being born of your cleanest light,
A place where the bonfires forge skies of purity,
Where the air links rings of contented perfume,
Where the water between two shores spreads warm bow-
    knots,
Where the earth is mother of cheeks and kisses.

If you yourselves want it, there is a place in the world,
There is a place beyond the burnings,
Farther than the pregnant wombs that plead with you
Through their cracks of mutilated cemeteries,
The sweet white kingdom of the star.

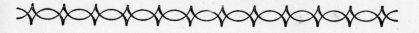

BIBLIOGRAPHY

General Works

PRESTON E. JAMES. Latin America. Boston, Lothrop, Lee & Stoddard, 1942.

HUBERT HERRING. Good neighbors. New Haven, Yale University Press, 1941.

G. DUNDAS CRAIG. The modernist trend in Spanish American poetry. Berkeley, University of California Press, 1934.

EDMUND WILSON. Axel's castle. New York, Scribner's, 1931.

GEORGE V. PLEKHANOV. Art and Society. Critics Group Pamphlet, No. 3. New York, 1936.

RENÉE TAUPIN. L'Influence de la symbolisme française sur la poesie américaine. Paris, Honoré Champion, 1929.

GUILLERMO DE TORRE. Literatura europea de vanguardia. Madrid, 1926.

SAMUEL PUTNAM. European caravan. New York, Brewer, Warren, & Putnam, 1931.

FEDRICO DE ONÍS SÁNCHEZ. Antología de la poesía española e hispanoamericana. Madrid, 1934. Anthology with introduction and notes.

ALBERTO TAURO. Presencia y definición del indigenismo literario, 3 (Lima, 1942), I, No. 8, 67–83.

J. URIEL GARCÍA. El nuevo indio. Cusco, 1937.

JORGE CARRERA ANDRADE. The new American and his point of view toward poetry (tr. by H. R. H.) Poetry (Chicago, 1943), LXII, No. 11, 88–105.

EMILIO BALLAGAS, Antología de poesía negra hispanoamericana. Madrid 1935. Anthology with critical introduction.

RAMÓN GUIRAO. Orbita de la poesía afrocubana 1928–37. Havana, 1938. Anthology with introduction and notes.

JOSÉ JUAN ARROM. La poesía afrocubana. Revista Iberoamericana (Mexico, 1942), IV, No. 8, 379–411.

ARTURO TORRES RÍOSECO. The epic of Latin American literature. New York, Oxford University Press, 1942.

Luis Alberto Sánchez, Historia de la literatura Americana (2nd ed.) Santiago de Chile, 1940.

Studies of Individual Poets

Ramón López Velarde

R. Lozano. La poesía criolla de Ramón López Velarde. *Prisma* (Madrid, 1922), II, No. 2, 96–110.

J. Torres Bodet. Cercanía de López Velarde. *Atenea* (Concepción, Chile, 1931), VIII, No. 71, 63–79.

E. González Rojo. Un discípulo de López Velarde. *Contemporáneos* (Mexico, 1928), I, No. 2, 215–224.

H. R. Hays. A Mexican symbolist. *Poetry* (Chicago, 1940), LVII, No. 1, 40–42.

See also introduction to El son del corazón by Genaro Fernández MacGregor and concluding essay to same volume by Rafael Cuevas, as well as the introduction to Poemas escogidos by Xavier Villaurutia.

Luis Carlos López

A. Llorente Arroyo. Luis Carlos López. *Hispania* (Stanford University, 1924), VII, 377–386.

F. García Godoy. La literatura de nuestros días. Madrid, 1915. Pp. 167–174.

Vicente Huidobro

H. S. Holmes. Huidobro and creationism. Institute of French Studies, Columbia University, New York, 1933.

Juan Arcos y Alberto Baeza Flores. Dos poetas chilenos. *América* (Havana), Nos. 1, 2, 3, 56–   , November-December, 1941.

See also Guillermo de Torre. Literatura europea de vanguardia.

Eugenio Florit

See introduction to Doble acento by Juan Ramón Jiménez.

Jorge Luis Borges

I. Pereda Valdés. Borges, poeta de Buenos Aires. *Nosotros* (Buenos Aires, 1926), LII, 106–109.

Jorge Carrera Andrade

PEDRO SALINAS. Registro de Jorge Carrera Andrade. Pub. of *Revista Iberoamericana*, Mexico, 1942.

ANTONIO DE UNDURRAGA. La órbita poética de Jorge Carrera Andrade. Pub. of *Revista Iberoamericana*, Mexico, 1942.

H. R. HAYS, Jorge Carrera Andrade, magician of metaphors. *Books Abroad* (Norman, Okla., 1943), XVII, No. 2, 101–105.

José Gorostiza

J. TORRES BODET. La poesía mexicana moderna. *El Sol* (Madrid), supplement of February, 1928.

Pablo de Rokha

OSCAR CHÁVEZ. El poeta crucificado. Santiago de Chile, 1940.

JUAN ARCOS Y ALBERTO BAEZA FLORES. Dos poetas chilenos. *América* (Havana), Nos. 1, 2, 3, pp. 56– , November-December, 1941.

Nicolás Guillén

REGINO E. BOTI. La poesía cubana de Nicolás Guillén. *Revista Bimestre Cubana* (1932), XXIX, No. 3, 243–253.

See also José Juan Arrom. La poesía afrocubana. *Revista Iberoamericana* (Mexico, 1942), IV, No. 8, 379–411.

Pablo Neruda

AMADO ALONSO. Pablo Neruda, poesía y estilo. Buenos Aires, 1940.

ARTURO ALDUNATE. El nuevo arte poético y Pablo Neruda. Santiago de Chile, 1936.

CONCHA MELÉNDEZ. Pablo Neruda en su extremo imperio. *Revista hispánica moderna* (New York, 1936), LII, No. 1, 1–34.

PABLO ROJAS PAZ. Pablo Neruda, la poesía y su inseguridad. *Nosotros* (Buenos Aires, 1937), No. 19, 121–134.

CLARENCE FINLAYSON. Poesía de Neruda, significacíon de elementos. *Universidad Católica Bolivariana* (Medellín, Colombia, 1940), V, Nos. 5–15, 17–48.

CLARENCE FINLAYSON. El problema de la muerte ontológica y la poesía de Pablo Neruda. *Idem* (1941), VI, Nos. 19–20, 299–319.

César Vallejo

J. BASADRE. Un poeta peruano. *Sierra* (Lima, 1928), II, Nos. 13–14, 30–34.

MANUEL BELTROY. Homenaje al poeta César Vallejo. *Garcilaso* (Lima, 1940), I, No. 1, 14–15.

MANUEL MORENO JIMENO. La noche de César Vallejo. *Idem*, pp. 18–19.

JUAN LARREA. Memoria de César Vallejo. *Idem*, pp. 20–22.

See also Estuardo Nuñez, Panorama actual de la poesía peruana (Lima, 1938), and introductory essays by Xavier Abril, José Bergamín, and Juan Larrea to Antología de César Vallejo, edited by Xavier Abril.

Jacinto Fombona Pachano

R. OLIVARES FIGUEROA. Nuevos poetas venezolanos. Caracas, 1939. Pp. 99–108.

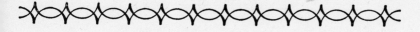

INDEX OF ENGLISH TITLES

INDEX OF SPANISH TITLES

DATE DUE

| NOV 7 72 | | | |
| NOV 1 6 1992 | | | |

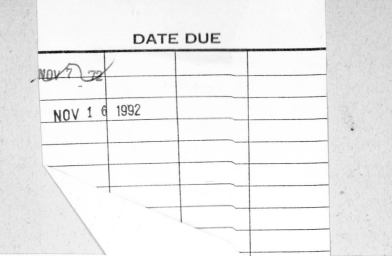

PQ
7084
H42   Hays, Hoffman R.
            12 Spanish Ame...   logy
         edited by H.R. Hay...   ons,
         notes, and introd. ...   Haven,
         Yale University Press...   rd, Ox-
         ford University Press,
            336p. 24cm.

            Poems in Spanish and Eng...   site pages.
            "Published on the founda...   shed in
         memory of Oliver Baty Cunnin [PRINTED IN U.S.A.] class of
         1917, Yale College."

247706   (Continued on next card)

(Continued on next card)

PQ   (card 2)
7084   Hays, Hoffman Reynolds, ed. 12 Spanish Ameri-
H42   can poets. 1943.

1.Spanish American poetry (Collections) 2.Spanish
American poetry-Translations into English. 3.English
poetry-Translations from Spanish. 4.Spanish American
poetry-Bio-bibl. I.Yale   University. Oliver Baty
Cunningham Memorial Publi-   cation Fund. II.Title.